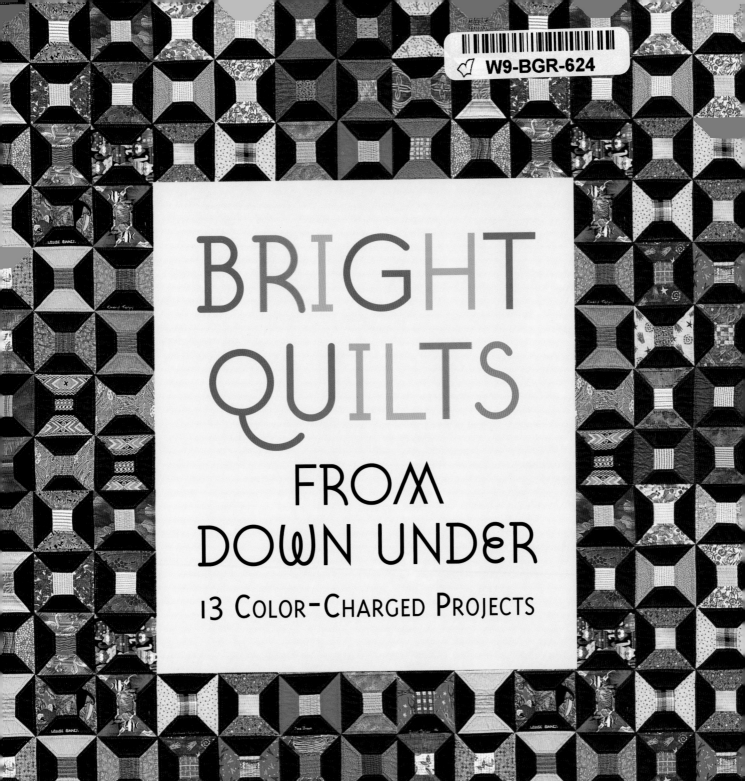

BRIGHT QUILTS

FROM DOWN UNDER

13 Color-Charged Projects

From "Australian Patchwork and Quilting" Magazine

Martingale®
& COMPANY

Bright Quilts from Down Under:
13 Color-Charged Projects
© 2003 Martingale & Company

That Patchwork Place® is an imprint of
Martingale & Company®.

Martingale & Company
20205 144th Avenue NE
Woodinville, WA 98072-8478
www.martingale-pub.com

The quilt designs in this book were originally
published by Express Publications Pty., Ltd.
Photographs courtesy of Express Publications.

Printed in China
08 07 06 05 04 03   8 7 6 5 4 3 2 1

CREDITS

President — Nancy J. Martin
CEO — Daniel J. Martin
Publisher — Jane Hamada
Editorial Director — Mary V. Green
Managing Editor — Tina Cook
Technical Editor — Karen Costello Soltys
Copy Editor — Melissa Bryan
Design Director — Stan Green
Illustrator — Robin Strobel
Cover and Text Designer — Shelly Garrison

Library of Congress Cataloging-in-Publication Data

Bright quilts from down under.
    p. cm.
    ISBN 1-56477-482-1
    1. Patchwork—Australia—Patterns.
    2. Quilting—Australia. 3. Patchwork quilts—Australia.

TT835.B6997 2003
746.46'041—dc21   2003004858

Mission Statement
Dedicated to providing quality products and service to inspire creativity.

CONTENTS

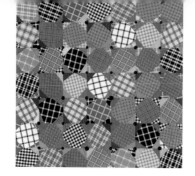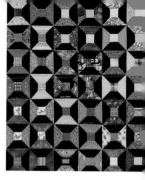

INTRODUCTION

Brightly colored fabrics are so popular with quiltmakers today. Walk into any quilt shop and you'll see a riot of color—bolts of hot pinks, chartreuses, electric blues, and more. Many of these fabrics are printed with juvenile themes that are perfect for brightening up any child's room. But you don't have to be a kid—just young at heart—to enjoy quilting with clear, pure colors.

For more adult tastes, there are many lovely batiks to choose from. Elegant prints with leaves, swirls, and other grown-up motifs abound, too. Even plaids are making a comeback, this time around with a touch of whimsy as they're woven in fun, crayon-box colors. Hand-dyed cottons are another wonderful way to add pizzazz to a project.

But now that you've found them, what do you do with all these intensely colored fabrics? Turn to *Bright Quilts from Down Under*. In a land of brilliant blue skies, aqua surf, and rich, red earth, it's no wonder that so many Australian quiltmakers are inspired to use such vividly appealing color schemes. The 13 patterns in this book range from very easy to more challenging, from whimsical to sophisticated, but they all have one thing in common—a big punch of color. Whether you're making the "I Spy" quilt for a youngster or the "Batik Nine Patch" for yourself, the result will be sure to satisfy your craving for color.

Karen Costello Soltys

Karen Costello Soltys
Editor

◀ Orange Delight

Bitz & Piecez ▶

◀ Batik Nine Patch

Isabella ▶

◀ Crazy Hearts

Floating Four Patch ▶

◀ Happy Hannah

I Spy ▶

◀ Five-Patch Cross

Friendship Spools ▶

◄ Square Dance

Amish Nine Patch ►

◀ Garden Gate

Finished quilt size: 46½" x 66½" (118 cm x 169 cm) • Finished block sizes: 8" (20 cm) and 2" (5 cm)

ORANGE DELIGHT

With its refreshing colors and effective design, Lisa Walton's scrap quilt is simply a delight to stitch. Lisa used scrap strips of her hand-dyed fabrics cut in uneven widths to create this vibrant lap quilt. The blocks are a fun interpretation of a traditional Log Cabin block, with a whimsy all their own.

MATERIALS

All yardages are based on 42"-wide (107 cm) fabric unless otherwise noted.

- 8 fat quarters of assorted purples and greens in varying tones of light, medium, and dark for blocks and binding
- 1⅛ yards (1 m) of yellow for sashing
- ½ yard (40 cm) of orange for block centers
- 3 yards (2.7 m) of backing fabric
- 52" x 72" (127 cm x 178 cm) piece of batting

CUTTING

All cutting dimensions include ¼" seam allowances.

From the orange fabric, cut:

- 3 strips, 4" x 42"; crosscut into 24 squares, 4" x 4"

From the assorted fat quarters, cut:

- 12 binding strips, 2½" x 20"
- Cut the remainder of the fat quarters into strips, varying from 1¼" to 2¼" wide. The strips do not need to have parallel edges.

From the yellow fabric, cut:

- 4 strips, 8½" x 42"; crosscut into 58 sashing strips, 2½" x 8½"

BLOCK CONSTRUCTION

The large blocks and the smaller sashing and border blocks are made in a similar fashion. You need 24 large blocks and 143 small blocks.

Large Blocks

The quilt shown has 8 purple blocks and 16 green blocks.

1. To make a purple block, sew a purple strip to one side of a 4" orange center square, right sides together. The block will gain visual interest if you sew at a slight angle as shown, rather than aligning the raw edges. Flip the strip open and press so that the seam is toward the purple strip. Then trim the excess fabric from the purple strip.

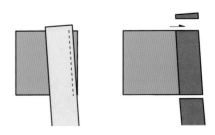

2 Using the same purple fabric, sew a strip to the opposite side of the center square. Press and trim as in step 1 on page 13. Again using the same fabric, add the top and bottom strips to create a complete round of logs around the orange center.

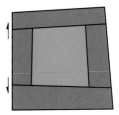

3 Using a different purple fabric, add the second round of strips in the same manner: side strips first and then the top and bottom strips. Add the third round of strips using yet another purple fabric. Trim the completed block to 8½" square.

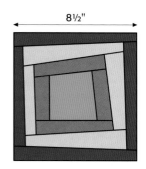

8½"

4 Repeat steps 1–3 until you have made 8 purple blocks. Then use the same steps to make 16 green blocks, also with orange centers.

Small Blocks

Each of the 35 sashing blocks has an orange center, but the centers vary in size. The additional small blocks are used for the borders, and their centers are a mix of orange, green, purple, and yellow.

1 For the sashing squares, use scraps of the orange fabric to cut center squares varying in size from 1½" to 2". Each square has one round of strips, either purple or green. The quilt shown has 15 purple sashing squares in the interior of the quilt and 20 green sashing squares around the perimeter. Sew one round of purple or green strips to each center square as you did for the large blocks. Trim the completed blocks to 2½" square.

2½"

2 For the border squares, use leftover bits of all colors for the block centers. They should measure between 1½" and 2" square. Sew one round of logs onto each center square, using the same color for all four sides of each block. Trim the completed blocks to 2½" square. Make a total of 108 border blocks.

2½"   2½"

Speedy Piecing

To make quick work of piecing the 143 small blocks, start with scrap squares and chain-piece them in a row to a scrap strip of fabric. Cut the pieces apart, and you're ready to chain-piece them along the next edge.

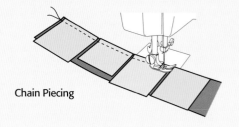

Chain Piecing

14

QUILT ASSEMBLY

1 Using a design wall or floor, lay out your large blocks and sashing strips in rows. The quilt is constructed in four vertical rows of six blocks each, with the sashing in between. The five sashing rows are each made up of seven small blocks with orange centers and six sashing strips. Each row begins and ends with a small block.

Quilt Assembly

2 Sew the blocks and sashing pieces together into rows. Press the seams toward the sashing strips.

3 Pin the rows together, carefully aligning the small squares in the sashing rows with the sashing strips in the block rows. Sew the rows together and press the quilt top.

BORDER

1 Sew the remaining small blocks together to make two lengths of 31 blocks each for the side borders. Make two lengths of 23 blocks each for the top and bottom borders. The side borders should measure 62½". and the top and bottom borders should be 46½".

2 Pin the side borders to the quilt top. You should have four small blocks aligned with each sashing strip. Sew the side borders to the quilt and press the seams toward the sashing strips.

3 Pin and then sew the top and bottom borders in place in the same manner. Again, press the seams toward the sashing strips.

FINISHING

1 Cut the backing fabric into two equal lengths. Piece the backing with a horizontal seam and trim it so that it is approximately 6" larger than the quilt top.

2 Layer the quilt top with the batting and backing; baste the layers together.

3 Hand or machine quilt as desired. Lisa hand quilted hers with diagonal lines in alternating directions. She started in the orange centers with the line on one diagonal and then changed the direction for each round of strips.

4 Trim the excess batting and backing fabric even with the edges of the quilt top. Join the assorted colors of binding strips with diagonal seams and use them to bind the edges of the quilt.

5 Label your quilt and attach a hanging sleeve, if desired.

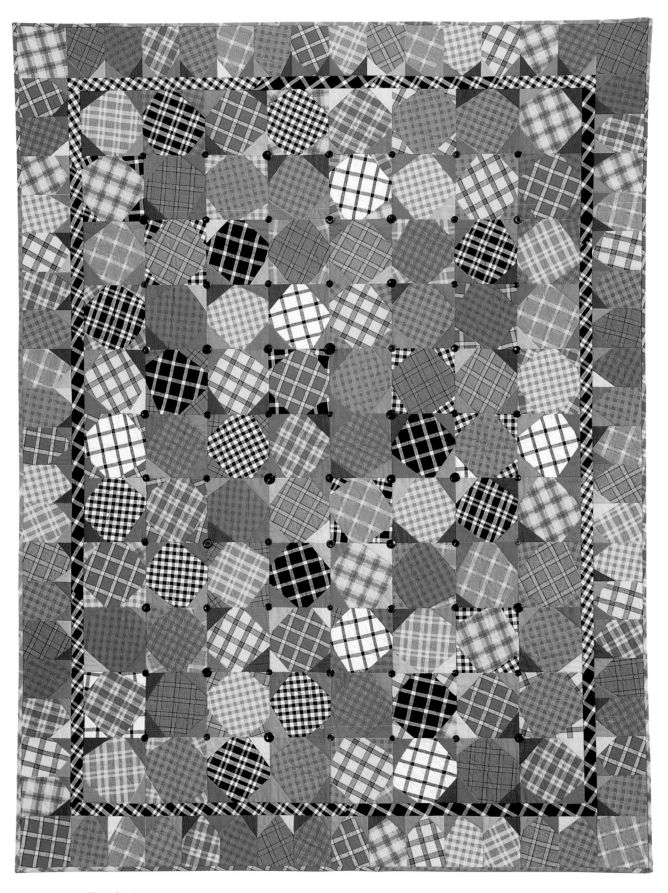

Finished quilt size: 55½" x 65½" (141 cm x 166 cm) • Finished block size: 5" (12.7 cm)

BITZ AND PIECEZ

Jan Mullen invites you to take risks with color and enjoy creating movement within a quilt, using her not-so-conventional cutting techniques on directional fabrics. The traditional Melon Patch block takes on a new look when you follow Jan's lead with crooked cutting and working off-center. It's hard to take your eyes off the result, which is a dance of color and movement. A narrow black-and-white check border sets off the color display, and black buttons stitched at the block intersections add even more fun.

MATERIALS

All yardages are based on 42"-wide (107 cm) fabric unless otherwise noted.

- ¼ yard (20 cm) *each* of 14 bright-color plaids for blocks, outer border, and binding
- ½ yard (50 cm) *each* of 4 black-and-white checks and plaids for blocks and inner border
- 13 fat eighths of bright solids (greens, yellows, blues, purples, and pinks) for blocks
- 3½ yards (3.2 m) of backing fabric
- 61" x 71" (160 cm x 190 cm) piece of batting
- 70 assorted black buttons

Working STARGAZEY Style

Quilt designer Jan Mullen is noted for her lopsided approach to patchwork, which started with her original and very popular "Stargazey" pattern. Here are some tips for working in her fun style:

- Cut and trim all fabric with a rotary cutter and ruler.
- It is not necessary to sew a perfect ¼"-wide seam when adding the corners of the Melon Patch blocks, but it is essential to sew a straight seam to keep your block flat.
- Press each seam after stitching it.
- Make up a sample block to see how the measurements work for you. Adapt your cutting and piecing to suit your desired result.
- Cut multiple layers at a time and use chain-piecing just as with traditional patchwork for quick and easy assembly.

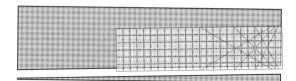

CUTTING

All cutting measurements include ¼" seam allowances. Instructions call for cutting strips across the width of the fabric; however, please note that Jan has cut all her plaid pieces on an angle to achieve her "crooked" look, as shown in the diagram below.

From the assorted bright-color and black-and-white plaids, cut:

- 15 strips, 5½" wide and on a slight bias; vary the angle from strip to strip. Crosscut the strips into 88 squares, 5½" x 5½".

From the assorted bright-color plaids, black-and-white plaids, and solids, cut:

- 176 squares, 3½" x 3½". Note that this measurement is flexible. Feel free to cut the squares a little larger, a little crooked, or off-square to add variety and character to your Melon Patch blocks. Cut each square in half once diagonally to yield 352 triangles.

From the black-and-white checks and plaids, cut:

- 5 strips, 1½" wide and slightly off grain

From the bright-color plaids, cut:

- 66 rectangles, 3½" x 4½"
- 4 squares, 4½" x 4½"
- Enough 2"-wide bias strips to total 255" of binding

From the assorted solids, cut:

- 66 squares, 2½" x 2½"; cut each square in half once diagonally to yield 132 triangles

BLOCK CONSTRUCTION

You need 88 Melon Patch blocks for this quilt. Jan used matching plaid corners for 37 blocks and corners of assorted solid colors for the remaining 51 blocks.

1 Select a 5½" square to use as the "melon," and place it right side up on your sewing table. Select a 3½" triangle and place it on a corner of the square,

right side up, with the corner of the triangle overlapping that of the underlying square as shown. Flip the triangle over so the pieces are now right sides together. *At the same time* push the triangle up toward the corner a little to account for the seam allowance. Stitch across the long edge of the triangle, and then flip it open and press it back over the seam line.

2 Turn your work over and trim the triangle even with the background square as shown. Then flip the unit back over to the right side, pull back the triangle to expose the excess background underneath, and trim this to a ¼" allowance.

Trim from wrong side of block.   Trim excess background.

3 Repeat for the other three corners of the square, trying to vary the triangle positions in each corner. One Melon Patch block is now complete. Repeat to make all 88 blocks.

Make 88 total.

QUILT ASSEMBLY

1 Lay out the blocks in 11 horizontal rows of 8 blocks each. Rearrange them until you are happy with the mix of color and fabrics.

❷ Stitch the blocks together into rows and press the seams of alternate rows in opposite directions. Stitch the rows together, butting the seams at the intersections of the blocks.

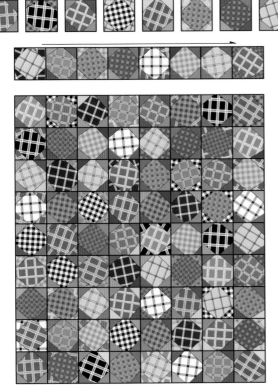

Quilt Assembly

BORDERS

❶ For the inner border, join the 1½"-wide black-and-white check and plaid strips, end to end, using diagonal seams. Press the seams open.

❷ From this long strip cut two strips, 55½" long, for the side borders. Stitch these to the opposite sides of the quilt top, with the black-and-white border strips underneath so that the feed dogs help control the stretch. Press the seams toward the border strips. Cut two strips, 42½" long, from the remaining length and then sew these strips to the top and bottom of the quilt top in the same manner.

❸ For the outer border, use the 3½" x 4½" rectangles as the melons. Stitch a 2½" triangle to two adjacent corners on one short end of each melon, as described in steps 1–3 of "Block Construction," opposite. Make 66 melon rectangles.

❹ Sew the melons together side by side to make the outer borders. Make two borders of 19 melons each for the sides of the quilt. Make sure that the small triangle corners are all along the same edge of the strip. Pin mark these strips and the sides of the quilt top into quarters. Join one strip to each side of the quilt top, matching the pins and ensuring that the small triangle corners are adjacent to the black-and-white inner border. Press the seams toward the black-and-white borders.

Side Border
Make 2.

❺ Make two more borders of 14 melons each for the top and bottom of the quilt. Join a 4½" plaid square to each end of both strips. Pin mark the strips and the top and bottom edges of the quilt top into quarters. Join the strips to the quilt top, matching the pins, and press the seams toward the black-and-white borders.

Top or Bottom Border
Make 2.

FINISHING

❶ Cut the backing fabric into two equal lengths. Piece the backing with a horizontal seam and trim it so that it is approximately 6" larger than the quilt top.

❷ Layer the quilt top with the batting and backing; baste the layers together.

❸ Hand or machine quilt as desired. Jan first machine quilted in the ditch around the border and the melons to stabilize the quilt top. Switching to freehand quilting, she then stitched large simple images of daisies, butterflies, suns, hearts, and her trademark "starz" to decorate the melons and to allow the unquilted corners to stand out. As a final touch, stitch a black button to every block intersection.

❹ Trim the excess batting and backing fabric even with the edges of the quilt top. Join the bright-color plaid binding strips with diagonal seams and use them to bind the edges of the quilt.

❺ Label your quilt and attach a hanging sleeve, if desired.

Finished quilt size: 64¼" x 77" (162 cm x 196 cm) • Finished block size: 4½" (11.5 cm)

BATIK NINE PATCH

One of Susan Mathews's all-time favorite quilt blocks is the timeless Nine Patch.
It is a simple yet effective block, and here Susan presents a beautiful example
of richly colored batik Nine Patches set on point against squares of
bright yellow hand-dyed fabric. The simplicity of the design
allows the drama of the fabrics to shine.

MATERIALS

*All yardages are based on 42"-wide (107 cm) fabric unless
otherwise noted.*

- 1¾ yards (1.6 m) of dark feather batik for squares
- 1¼ yards (1.1 m) of bright yellow hand-dyed fabric
  for squares and setting triangles
- 1⅛ yards (90 cm) of medium-light fish batik for Nine
  Patch blocks and squares
- ⅞ yard (80 cm) of light batik for Nine Patch blocks
- ¾ yard (70 cm) of dark solid batik for Nine Patch
  blocks
- ¾ yard (70 cm) of medium floral batik for squares
- ⅝ yard (50 cm) of dark batik for binding
- 4⅝ yards (4.2 m) of backing fabric
- 70" x 83" (178 cm x 211 cm) piece of batting

CUTTING

All cutting dimensions include ¼" seam allowances.

From the light batik (A), cut:

- 13 strips, 2" x 42"

From the medium floral batik (B), cut:

- 3 strips, 2" x 42"
- 4 strips, 5" x 42"; crosscut into 32 squares, 5" x 5"

From the medium-light fish batik (C), cut:

- 8 strips, 2" x 42"
- 3 strips, 5" x 42"; crosscut into 20 squares, 5" x 5"

From the dark solid batik (D), cut:

- 8 strips, 2" x 42"

From the yellow hand-dyed fabric (E), cut:

- 3 strips, 5" x 42"; crosscut into 24 squares, 5" x 5"
- 2 strips, 7⅞" x 42"; crosscut into 10 squares,
  7⅞" x 7⅞". Cut each square in half twice diagonally
  to yield 40 setting triangles.
- 2 squares, 5⅝" x 5⅝"; cut each square in half once
  diagonally to yield 4 corner triangles

From the dark feather batik (F), cut:

- 9 strips, 5" x 42"; crosscut into 71 squares, 5" x 5"

From the dark batik for binding, cut:

- 8 strips, 2¼" x 42"

BLOCK CONSTRUCTION

This quilt uses four different colorations of the basic Nine Patch. You need a total of 72 blocks: 4 of block 1, 20 of block 2, 40 of block 3, and 8 of block 4.

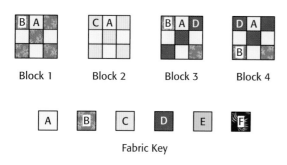

Block 1 Block 2 Block 3 Block 4

Fabric Key

1 To make block 1 you need two strips each of light batik (A) and floral batik (B). Cut the strips in half crosswise to yield four pieces of each color. You'll use only three. Sew the strips together along the long edges as shown to make two different strip sets. Cut 2"-wide segments from the strip sets: eight segments from strip set B-A-B and four segments from strip set A-B-A. Sew the segments together to make four of block 1.

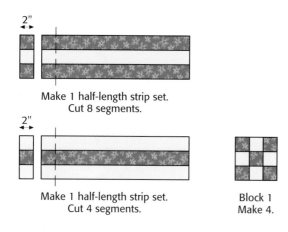

2"

Make 1 half-length strip set.
Cut 8 segments.

2"

Make 1 half-length strip set.
Cut 4 segments.

Block 1
Make 4.

2 To make block 2 you need three strips each of light batik (A) and medium-light batik (C). Sew the strips together along the long edges to make two different strip sets as shown. Make two of strip set

C-A-C and cut forty 2"-wide segments from it. Make one of strip set A-C-A and cut twenty 2"-wide segments from it. Sew the segments together to make 20 of block 2.

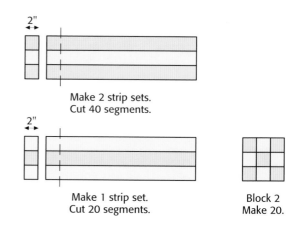

2"

Make 2 strip sets.
Cut 40 segments.

2"

Make 1 strip set.
Cut 20 segments.

Block 2
Make 20.

3 To make block 3 you need six light (A) strips, six dark solid (D) strips, and four medium floral (B) strips. Sew the strips together along the long edges to make four of strip set B-A-D. Cut eighty 2"-wide segments from these strip sets. Sew the remaining strips together to create two of strip set A-D-A. Cut forty 2"-wide segments from these strip sets. Sew the segments together to make 40 of block 3.

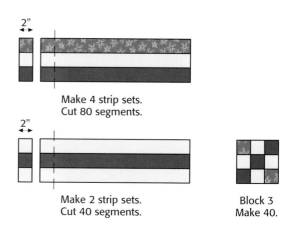

2"

Make 4 strip sets.
Cut 80 segments.

2"

Make 2 strip sets.
Cut 40 segments.

Block 3
Make 40.

4 To make block 4 you need two light (A) strips, two dark solid (D) strips, and one medium floral (B) strip. Sew the strips together along the long edges to make one of strip set D-A-B. Cut sixteen 2"-wide segments from this strip set. Cut the remaining A and D strips in half crosswise. Make an A-D-A strip set using these strips. Cut eight 2"-wide segments from this strip set. Sew the segments together to make eight of block 4.

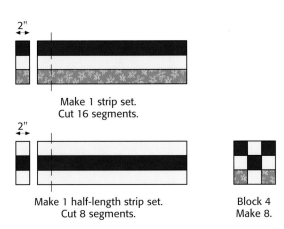

Make 1 strip set.
Cut 16 segments.

Make 1 half-length strip set.
Cut 8 segments.

Block 4
Make 8.

QUILT ASSEMBLY

1 Arrange the fabric squares and Nine Patch blocks in rounds, working from the center outward. Refer to the round-by-round layout in the quilt assembly diagram, right, and also to the quilt photograph on page 20.

Round 1: 1 square of fabric F (dark feather batik)

Round 2: 4 of block 1

Round 3: 8 squares of fabric C (medium-light batik)

Round 4: 8 of block 3, and 4 of block 4 for the corners

Round 5: 16 squares of fabric F (dark feather batik)

Round 6: 20 of block 2

Round 7: 24 squares of fabric E (bright yellow)

Round 8: Extension row that converts the square quilt top into a rectangle and uses 12 squares of fabric C (medium-light batik) on the top and bottom only

Round 9: 14 squares of fabric F (dark feather batik) on the top and bottom only

Round 10: 32 squares of fabric B (medium floral batik)

Round 11: 32 of block 3, and 4 of block 4 for the corners

Round 12: 40 squares of fabric F (dark feather batik)

Round 13: 40 setting triangles and 4 corner triangles in fabric E (bright yellow)

2 Once the blocks are arranged properly, sew them together in diagonal rows. Press the seams for each alternate row in the opposite direction.

3 Sew the diagonal rows together and press the quilt top.

Quilt Assembly

FINISHING

1 Cut the backing fabric into two equal lengths and cut one of the pieces in half lengthwise. Sew the narrower strips to either side of the full-width piece to make a backing with two vertical seams. Trim the backing so that it is approximately 6" larger than the quilt top.

2 Layer the quilt top with the batting and backing; baste the layers together.

3 Hand or machine quilt as desired. Susan suggests quilting through the diagonals of the squares and Nine Patch blocks. If you are machine quilting, she suggests quilting in the ditch along all the seam lines first. Some rows of squares could have a simple pattern repeated in each square.

4 Trim the excess batting and backing fabric even with the edges of the quilt top. Join the dark binding strips with diagonal seams and use them to bind the edges of the quilt.

5 Label your quilt and attach a hanging sleeve, if desired.

Finished quilt size: 90" x 90" (229 cm square) • Finished block size: 18½" x 21" (47 cm x 53 cm)

ISABELLA

What a cheery appliqué project! Bouquets of flowers and clouds
of butterflies seem to dance over the surface of this quilt designed by Melanie Coutts.
It's simply perfect for a little girl's room. Melanie used contrasting colors
to enhance the brightness of this quilt. When you are selecting your own fabrics
for this project, consider the recipient's favorite colors. Other contrasting
combinations would work just as well, such as bright primaries
(red, yellow, and blue), or electric blue and sizzling orange.

MATERIALS

All yardages are based on 42"-wide (107 cm) fabric unless otherwise noted.

- ¼ yard (20 cm) or fat quarter *each* of 10 bright tone-on-tone fabrics for appliqués and pieced sashing

- ¼ yard (20 cm) or fat quarter *each* of 10 bright prints for fourth border

- 1¾ yards (1.6 m) of bright pink mottled fabric for second and sixth borders

- 1¼ yards (1.1 m) of bright green mottled fabric for third border

- ⅔ yard (60 cm) each of 4 light tone-on-tone fabrics (orange, pink, green, and yellow) for appliqué block backgrounds

- ½ yard (40 cm) of yellow checked fabric for first border

- ½ yard (40 cm) of bright orange mottled fabric for fifth border

- ⅓ yard (30 cm) each of 4 medium-light tone-on-tone fabrics (pink, lavender, green, and orange) for block frames

- ⅓ yard (30 cm) each of 3 green fabrics for stems, leaves, and flower buds

- 12" x 12" (30 cm square) piece each of 4 bright fabrics for watering can, bucket, flowerpot, and wheelbarrow appliqués

- 1 yard (90 cm) of bright yellow print for binding

- 8¼ yards (7.6 m) of backing fabric

- 96" x 96" (244 cm square) piece of batting

- Brown embroidery floss

- Template plastic

- Chalk pencil

- Fine-point permanent marking pen

CUTTING

All cutting dimensions include ¼" seam allowances.

From *each* of the 4 light tone-on-tone fabrics, cut:

- 1 rectangle, 19" x 21½"

From *each* of the 4 medium-light tone-on-tone fabrics, cut:

- 2 strips, 2" x 19"
- 2 strips, 3¼" x 24½"

From the 10 bright tone-on-tone fabrics, cut:

- 81 squares, 4½" x 4½". Save the remaining bright fabrics for cutting appliqués.

From the yellow checked fabric, cut:

- 8 strips, 1½" x 42"

From the bright pink fabric, cut:

- 8 strips, 1" x 42"
- 9 strips, 4½" x 42"

From the bright green fabric, cut:

- 8 strips, 4½" x 42"

From the 10 bright prints, cut:

- 72 squares, 4½" x 4½"
- 8 rectangles, 1½" x 4½"

From the bright orange fabric, cut:

- 8 strips, 1½" x 42"

From the bright yellow print, cut:

- 10 binding strips, 3" x 42"

From the assorted green fabrics, cut:

- 29 bias strips, ¾" x 12"

BLOCK CONSTRUCTION

① Fold the 19" x 21½" background rectangles in half once vertically and once horizontally, and press them lightly to create guidelines for the appliqué placement. Enlarge each block design 225% as indicated on the patterns on pages 29–32. Then, using a light box or window, position the pattern designs and trace them onto the background using a pencil or water-soluble pen.

② Using a fine-point permanent marking pen, trace all the patterns for each block onto template plastic. Label the templates and cut them out. To avoid confusing the many pieces, keep the templates for each block in a separate plastic bag.

③ Use the templates and the remaining scraps of the bright tone-on-tone fabrics to prepare the shapes for your favorite method of appliqué. Use the 12" squares of bright fabrics to prepare a bucket, watering can, wheelbarrow, and flowerpot for appliqué. If you choose fusible appliqué, you will need to flip the templates over when you trace the shapes onto fusible web so that the finished design matches the quilt shown. If you prefer hand appliqué, note that the patterns do not include seam allowances. For the bias stems, turn under a scant ¼" seam allowance as you appliqué the stems in place. Adjust the length of the stems as required to fit each position. For the specific number of pieces to cut for each appliqué block, see below.

Block A: Cut 7 tulips, 6 posies and posy centers, 2 buds, 15 stems, 6 leaves, and 1 bucket and handle, using the block pattern on page 29. Place the stems and leaves on the block and pin them in place. Then pin the flowers and bucket on top, referring to the quilt photograph for placement. Begin by appliquéing the stems and the leaves. Where the appliqué pieces overlap, leave the seam allowance unturned to reduce bulk. Make and appliqué the buds, again following the quilt photo. Then appliqué the flowers, adding a bright center in a contrasting color. Finally, appliqué the bucket, ensuring all the ends of the stems and leaves are tucked under the top rim of it.

Block B: Cut four large butterflies, four small butterflies, one dragonfly, one sunflower and sunflower center, and one watering can, using the block pattern on page 30. Position the watering can, sunflower, sunflower center, butterflies, and dragonfly on the block. Appliqué the lower wings on the butterflies first, followed by the upper wings, and then the bodies. Appliqué the body of the dragonfly, the lower wings, and the upper wings. Stem stitch all the antennae using two strands of brown embroidery floss.

Block C: Cut four large butterflies, two bees, three medium butterflies, one insect, one small butterfly, one wheelbarrow wheel, and one wheelbarrow, using the block pattern on page 31. Appliqué the block in the same manner as block B. To make the two bees and the insect, appliqué the wings over the bodies and add two rows of satin stitching, using two strands of brown embroidery floss across the lower section of the bees' bodies.

Block D: Cut 7 tulips, 5 posies and posy centers, 2 buds, 14 stems, 6 leaves, and 1 flowerpot, using the block pattern on page 32. Complete as for block A.

4 To frame the blocks, stitch a 2" x 19" strip to each side of the blocks, referring to the quilt photo for suggested color combinations. Press the seams toward the framing strips. Then join the 3¼" x 24½" strips of the same color to the top and bottom of the blocks and press.

APPLIQUÉD SASHING

1 Using the heart, circle, and square patterns on page 33, prepare 81 appliqué shapes for your favorite method of appliqué.

2 Place each appliqué shape on one of the 4½" bright tone-on-tone squares, pairing contrasting fabrics. For instance, place a pink heart on a green square or a yellow circle on a purple square. You may plan the layout of shapes in your quilt, or simply select them randomly as you go. Appliqué or fuse the shapes to the squares.

3 Using the quilt photograph on page 24 as a guide, join the 81 appliquéd squares into six strips of 6 squares each and three strips of 15 squares each. Press all seams in the same direction.

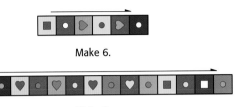

Make 6.

Make 3.

4 Lay out the four appliquéd blocks and the appliquéd strip sets. Sew the short strips to the opposite sides of each block, and then join the blocks to form two rows. Add the three longer strip sets above, between, and below the two rows, and press the seams toward the strips.

Quilt Assembly

Borders

This quilt has a series of six borders. The fourth border is pieced from squares and a few rectangles, while the others are made from long strips of fabric.

First Border

1 Join the eight 1½"-wide yellow checked strips end to end in pairs using diagonal seams. Trim and press the seams open.

2 Measure the length of the quilt top through the center and trim two of the border strips to this measurement, which should be approximately 60½". Attach the borders to the sides of the quilt top, easing as necessary. Press the seams toward the borders.

3 Measure the width of the quilt top through the center and trim the remaining two border strips to this measurement, which should be approximately 62½". Attach these borders to the top and bottom of the quilt top, easing if necessary and pressing as in step 2, above.

Second Border

Join the eight 1"-wide bright pink strips in pairs and press them as for the first border. Measure the quilt as described above, and then trim and attach the borders to the quilt in the same manner.

Third Border

Join the eight bright green strips in pairs and measure, trim, sew, and press as for the two previous borders.

Fourth Border

1 Stitch the 72 bright print 4½" squares into four strips of 17 squares each. (You will have 4 squares left over.) Join a 1½" x 4½" bright print rectangle to each end of all the border strips. Press all seams in one direction.

2 Sew two of the strips to the sides of the quilt top. Press the seams away from the pieced border.

3 Join a bright print square to each end of the two remaining pieced borders. Sew these borders to the top and bottom of the quilt and press as for the side borders.

Fifth Border

The fifth border is made using the bright orange strips. Piece the strips, measure the quilt top, and attach the border strips as for the first, second, and third borders.

Sixth Border

The sixth border is made using the nine 4½"-wide bright pink strips. Sew the strips together in pairs as for the other borders. Cut the remaining strip into quarters and sew one of these segments to each long strip. Measure the quilt top, trim the borders to fit, and attach the strips as for the previous borders. Press the completed quilt top.

Finishing

1 Cut the backing fabric into three equal lengths and sew the pieces together to make a backing with two vertical seams. Trim the backing so that it is approximately 6" larger than the quilt top.

2 Layer the quilt top with the batting and backing; baste the layers together.

3 Hand or machine quilt as desired. Melanie chose to hand quilt with a bright-colored quilting thread around each appliqué piece in the blocks. She stitched parallel lines about ½" apart on the wheelbarrow, and she outline quilted the borders ⅛" away from the seam lines. The third border features a quilting design of large interlocking hearts, while quilted circles, squares, and hearts (traced from the appliqué patterns) add character to the squares of the pieced border.

4 Trim the excess batting and backing fabric even with the edges of the quilt top. Join the bright yellow binding strips with diagonal seams and use them to bind the edges of the quilt.

5 Label your quilt and attach a hanging sleeve, if desired.

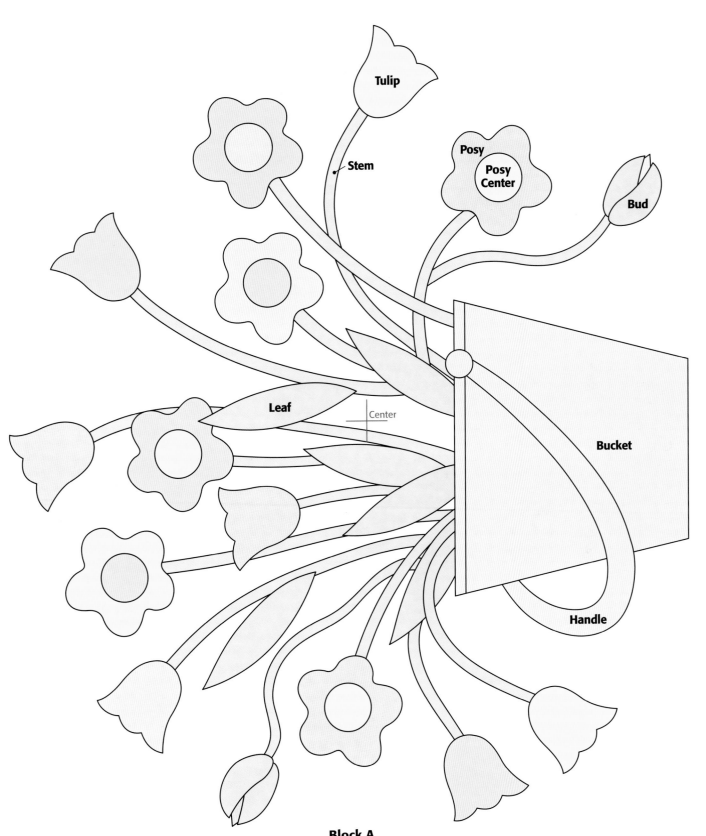

Block A
Enlarge pattern 225%.
Add seam allowances for hand appliqué.

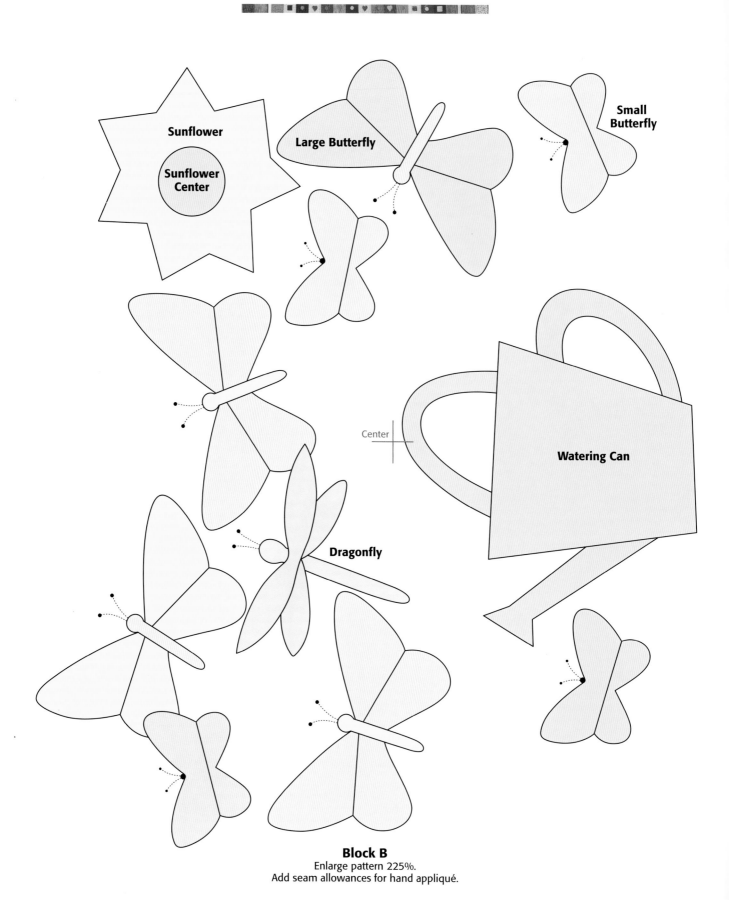

Sunflower

Sunflower Center

Large Butterfly

Small Butterfly

Center

Watering Can

Dragonfly

Block B
Enlarge pattern 225%.
Add seam allowances for hand appliqué.

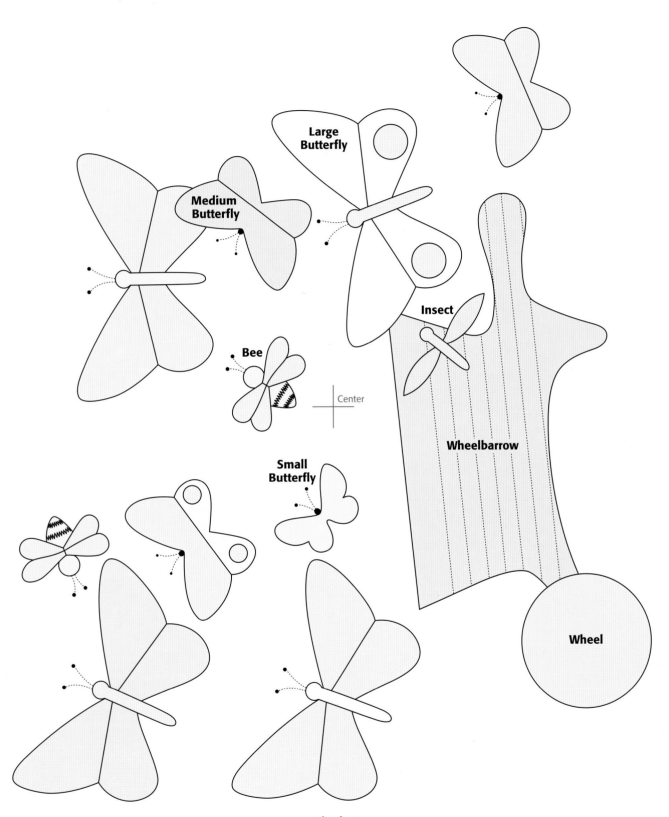

Block C
Enlarge pattern 225%.
Add seam allowances for hand appliqué.

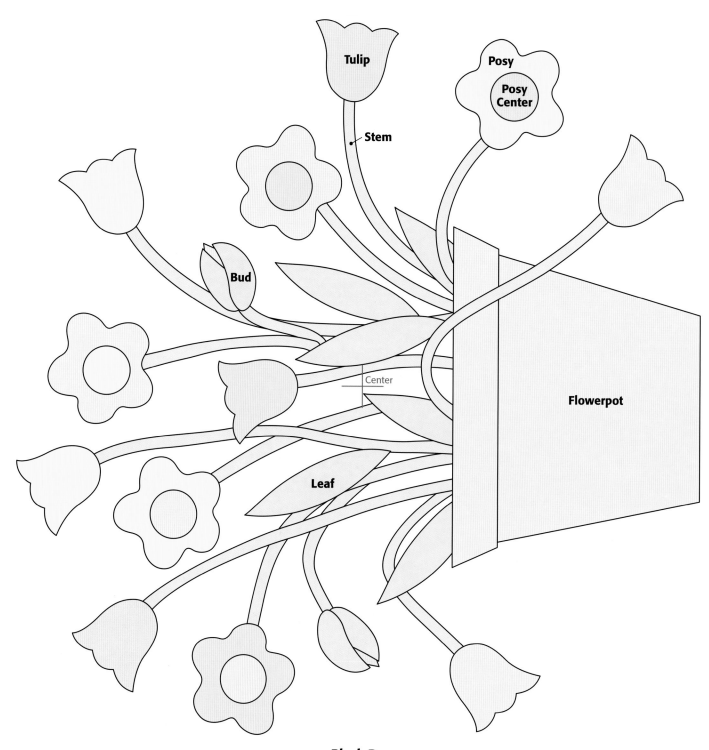

Block D
Enlarge pattern 225%.
Add seam allowances for hand appliqué.

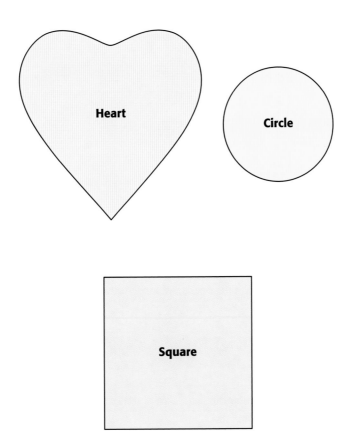

Heart

Circle

Square

Sashing Appliqué Patterns
Do not enlarge. Patterns on this page are 100%.
Add seam allowances for hand appliqué.

Finished quilt size: 51" x 74" (129.5 cm x 188 cm) • Finished block size: 10" (25 cm)

CRAZY HEARTS

This bright quilt by Joy White is a delight with its brilliant appliqué hearts. A lively sheet of decoupage paper provided the inspiration, but since Joy doesn't do decoupage she decided to make a quilt instead. She loved the strong, vivid colors and the simplicity of the design, and says it's proof that you can't beat hearts as a theme for a quilt. Cuddle someone you love in this generous-sized lap quilt, or add more blocks for a wonderfully colorful bed quilt.

MATERIALS

All yardages are based on 42"-wide (107 cm) fabric unless otherwise noted.

- 24 bright-color fat quarters (pinks, blues, greens, yellows, oranges, and purples) for hearts, block backgrounds, block borders, and sashing
- ½ yard (50 cm) of pink print for inner border
- ⅜ yard (30 cm) of blue print for sashing squares and outer border
- ½ yard (50 cm) of blue striped fabric for binding
- 3½ yards (3.2 m) of backing fabric
- 57" x 80" (145 cm x 203 cm) piece of batting
- Template plastic
- Freezer paper or fusible web
- Fine-point permanent marker

Blanket-Stitched Edges

The large hearts in this quilt will lend themselves quite nicely to a bit of decorative stitching. For a folksy look, consider stitching around each heart in a contrasting-color thread with a hand or machine blanket stitch or featherstitch. The stitching will add a touch of whimsy to the quilt, and also keep fused hearts in place, especially during machine washings.

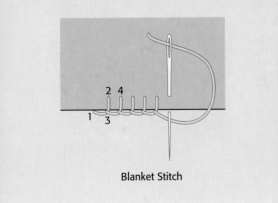

Blanket Stitch

CUTTING

All cutting dimensions include ¼" seam allowances.

From *each* of the 24 bright-color fat quarters, cut:

- 1 strip, 7½" x 20"; from each strip cut 1 square, 7½" x 7½". Reserve the remaining bright fabrics for the heart appliqués.

From *each* of 12 of the bright-color fat quarters, cut:

- 2 strips, 1" x 7½" (block A)
- 2 strips, 1" x 8½" (block A)
- 2 strips, 1" x 9½" (block B)
- 2 strips, 1" x 10½" (block B)
- 58 strips, 2" x 6¼"

From *each* of the other 12 bright-color fat quarters, cut:

- 2 strips, 1½" x 7½" (block B)
- 2 strips, 1½" x 9½" (block B)
- 2 strips, 1½" x 8½" (block A)
- 2 strips, 1½" x 10½" (block A)
- 58 strips, 2" x 6¼"

From the blue print, cut:

- 2 strips, 2" x 42"; crosscut into 35 squares, 2" x 2"
- 7 strips, 1" x 42"

From the pink print, cut:

- 7 strips, 1½" x 42"

From the blue striped fabric, cut:

- 7 binding strips, 2" x 42"

BLOCK CONSTRUCTION

❶ Make a plastic template of the heart pattern on page 39. Use the template to prepare 24 assorted bright hearts for your favorite method of appliqué. If you choose fusible appliqué, there is no need to add a seam allowance. For freezer-paper or needle-turn appliqué, you will need to add a scant ¼" seam allowance to each heart. The dashed lines on the heart pattern will help you center the hearts on the background fabrics.

❷ Fold the 24 background squares once vertically and once horizontally, and crease lightly to mark their centers. Using the center lines marked on the template, position the heart shapes on the background blocks and pin them in place. Fuse or stitch each heart in place. If you're using freezer-paper appliqué, carefully slash the background fabric behind the heart to remove the freezer paper. Press the completed blocks.

❸ Divide your blocks into two piles of 12 blocks each. Half of the blocks will be A blocks with a 1" border followed by a 1½" border. The other half will be B blocks with a 1½" border followed by a 1" border. The A and B blocks are alternated in the quilt layout, so you may want to determine your layout before choosing which fabric hearts will become A or B blocks.

Block A
Make 12.

Block B
Make 12.

4 For block A, stitch matching 1" x 7½" strips to opposite sides of the blocks, and press the seam allowances toward the blocks. Stitch matching 1" x 8½" strips to the top and bottom of the blocks and press the seams toward the strips.

5 For the outer round, choose strips that contrast with the first round. Sew 1½" x 8½" strips to the sides and then 1½" x 10½" strips to the top and bottom of the blocks in the same manner as for the narrow strips.

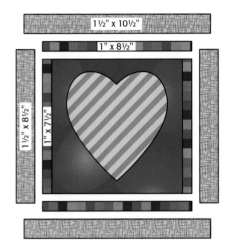

Block A Assembly

6 For block B, stitch matching 1½" x 7½" strips to opposite sides of the blocks, and press the seams toward the strips. Then add matching 1½" x 9½" strips to the top and bottom of the blocks and press the seams toward the strips. Join the contrasting narrow strips for the outer round in the same manner, using 1" x 9½" strips for the sides and 1" x 10½" strips for the top and bottom. All the blocks should measure 10½" x 10½".

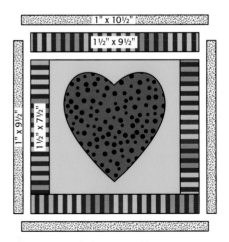

Block B Assembly

QUILT ASSEMBLY

1 The quilt blocks are separated by rows of colorful pieced sashing. To make each sashing strip, join two 2" x 6¼" strips of different colors with a diagonal seam as shown. Trim the excess fabric to leave a ¼" seam and press the seam toward the darker fabric. Then trim the resulting strip to 10½" long. Make a total of 58 sashing strips.

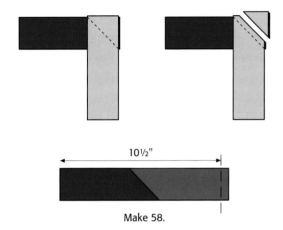

10½"

Make 58.

2 Lay out the blocks in six rows of four blocks each, referring to the quilt photograph on page 34. Be sure to alternate the placement of A and B blocks. Arrange pieced sashing strips and blue sashing squares between the blocks.

3 Sew the blocks and vertical sashing strips together into rows. Press the seams toward the sashing strips. Then sew the horizontal sashing strips and sashing squares together into rows, again pressing the seams toward the sashing strips.

4 Stitch the rows together, carefully matching the seam intersections. Press the seams toward the sashing strips.

Quilt Assembly

BORDERS

1 For the inner border, join the seven 1½" x 42" pink strips end to end to make one long strip.

2 Measure the length of the quilt top through the center and cut two borders from the long strip to this measurement, which should be approximately 71". Stitch the borders to the sides of the quilt, easing as necessary. Press the seams toward the borders.

3 Measure the width of the quilt top through the center and cut two borders from the remaining pieced strip to this measurement, which should be approximately 50". Sew the borders to the top and bottom of the quilt and press the seams toward the borders.

4 For the outer border, join the seven 1" x 42" blue strips end to end to make one long strip.

5 Measure and cut the side borders in the same manner as for the inner border. This measurement should be approximately 73". Join the borders to the sides of the quilt top and press the seams toward the blue borders.

6 Measure the quilt width in the same manner as for the inner border and cut two strips to this measurement, which should be approximately 51". Join these borders to the top and bottom of the quilt and press the seams toward the blue borders.

FINISHING

1 Cut the backing fabric into two equal lengths and sew the pieces together to make a backing with a horizontal seam. Trim the backing so that it is approximately 6" larger than the quilt top.

2 Layer the quilt top with the batting and backing; baste the layers together.

3 Hand or machine quilt as desired. Joy's quilt was professionally machine quilted with an allover loop pattern.

4 Trim the excess batting and backing fabric even with the edges of the quilt top. Join the blue striped binding strips with diagonal seams and use them to bind the edges of the quilt.

5 Label your quilt and attach a hanging sleeve, if desired.

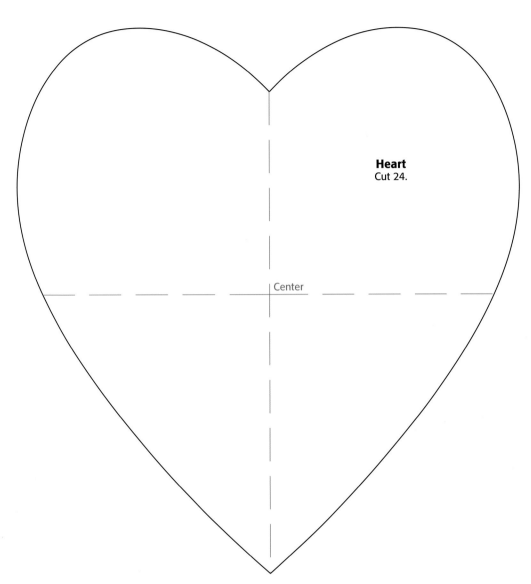

Heart
Cut 24.

Center

Add seam allowance for hand appliqué.

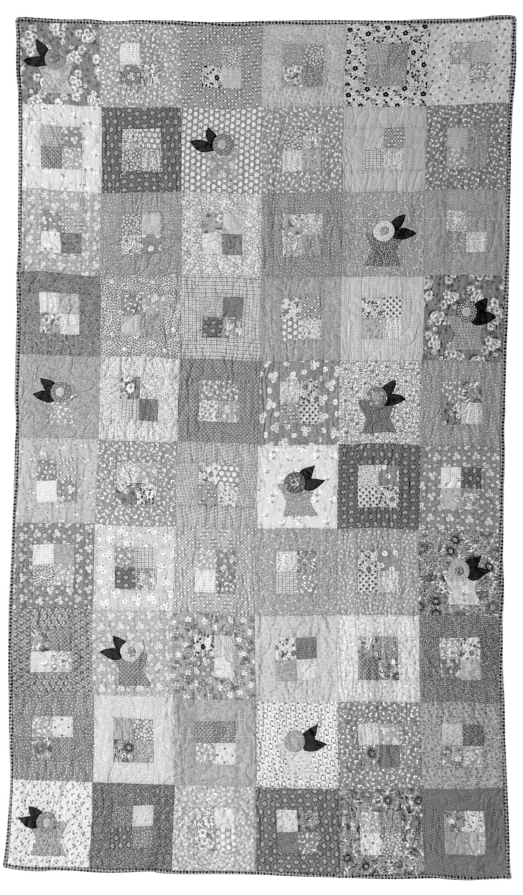

Finished quilt size: 48½" x 80½" (122 cm x 203 cm) • Finished block size: 8" (20 cm)

FLOATING FOUR PATCH

Lovely little appliqué basket blocks float between easy-to-make
Four Patch blocks on this scrap quilt. Quiltmaker Joanne Knott chose cheerful
1930s-style reproduction print fabrics for her design. While the result is quite colorful,
Joanne suggests the quilt could be just as effective made with plaids and
checks or in shades of pinks and blues for a baby quilt.

MATERIALS

All yardages are based on 42"-wide (107 cm) fabric unless otherwise noted.

- ⅛ yard (12 cm) *each* of 49 assorted prints for pieced blocks and appliqué baskets and flowers (If using scraps, you can substitute 49 assorted 12" [30 cm] squares.)
- 11 squares, 10" x 10" (25 cm x 25 cm), of assorted prints for appliqué backgrounds
- ⅛ yard (12 cm) or scraps of green for appliqué leaves
- ⅔ yard (60 cm) of green check for binding
- 4⅝ yards (4.2 m) of backing fabric
- 55" x 87" (140 cm x 221 cm) piece of batting
- Freezer paper or fusible web (optional)

CUTTING

All cutting dimensions include ¼" seam allowances. Patterns for the basket, flower, flower center, and leaf are on page 43.

From *each* of the 49 assorted prints, cut:

- 2 rectangles, 2½" x 4½"
- 2 rectangles, 2½" x 8½"
- 4 squares, 2½" x 2½"

From the leftover print fabrics, cut:

- 11 baskets
- 11 flowers
- 11 flower centers

From the assorted print squares, cut:

- 11 squares, 8½" x 8½"

From the green fabric, cut:

- 22 leaves

From the green check, cut:

- 7 binding strips, 2½" x 42"

BLOCK CONSTRUCTION

You need 49 Four Patch blocks and 11 appliqué basket blocks for this quilt.

Floating Four Patch Blocks

1. Sew the 2½" print squares together in pairs, selecting the colors randomly. Press the seams to one side and then sew the pairs together to complete 49 Four Patch units.

2. Stitch matching pairs of 2½" x 4½" rectangles to opposite sides of each Four Patch unit. Press the seams toward the rectangles. Stitch the two matching 2½" x 8½" rectangles to the remaining sides of each block and press the seams toward the rectangles. Repeat for all 49 blocks.

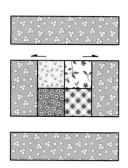

Make 49.

Appliqué Basket Blocks

1. Prepare 11 baskets, 11 flowers and flower centers, and 22 leaves for your favorite appliqué method, using the patterns opposite. Note that the patterns do not include seam allowance. If you choose to do hand appliqué, you'll need to add a scant ¼" seam allowance when cutting out the pieces.

2. Using the patterns as a placement guide, appliqué the pieces to the background squares. Make a total of 11 basket blocks.

Make 11.

QUILT ASSEMBLY

1. Referring to the quilt photograph on page 40 and the quilt assembly diagram below, arrange the 49 Floating Four Patch blocks and the 11 appliqué basket blocks in 10 rows of 6 blocks each. Rearrange the blocks until you are pleased with the color distribution. Feel free to move the appliqué blocks where you'd like.

2. Stitch the rows of blocks together and press the seams in alternate rows in opposite directions. Stitch the rows together and press the quilt top.

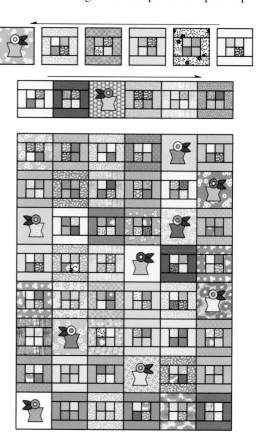

Quilt Assembly

FINISHING

1 Cut the backing fabric into three equal lengths. Piece the backing fabric with two horizontal seams and trim it so that it is approximately 6" larger than the quilt top.

2 Layer the quilt top with the batting and backing; baste the layers together.

3 Hand or machine quilt as desired. Joanne's quilt was machine quilted in a random allover pattern.

4 Trim the excess batting and backing fabric even with the edges of the quilt top. Join the green check binding strips with diagonal seams and use them to bind the edges of the quilt.

5 Label your quilt and attach a hanging sleeve, if desired.

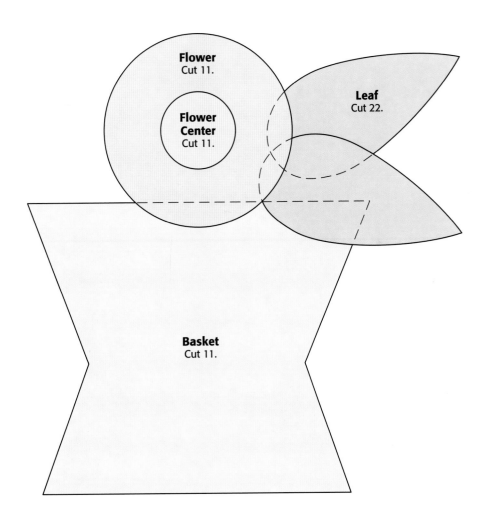

Flower
Cut 11.

Flower Center
Cut 11.

Leaf
Cut 22.

Basket
Cut 11.

Finished quilt size: 57½" x 81½" (146 cm x 207 cm) • Finished block size: 12" (30.5 cm)

HAPPY HANNAH

Blue skies and sunshine inspired Natasha Castelijn's quilt,
made for her daughter Hannah. This cheerful quilt is a fabric collector's dream.
An excellent exercise in color and balance, Natasha's use of bright, sunny fabrics
gives the age-old tradition of scrap quilts a totally modern feel.

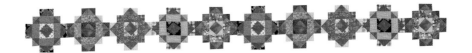

MATERIALS

All yardages are based on 42"-wide (107 cm) fabric unless otherwise noted.

- 2½ yards (2.1 m) of white-on-white print for background

- 1¾ yards (1.6 m) of blue print for blocks, first border, and binding

- ⅛ yard (12 cm) *each* of 50 assorted bright prints (If using scraps, you can substitute 50 assorted 12" [30 cm] squares.)

- 4⅞ yards (4.5 m) of backing fabric

- 64" x 88" (163 cm x 224 cm) piece of batting

CUTTING

All cutting dimensions include ¼" seam allowances. Each block requires six fabrics: blue print (A), white print (B), and four bright colors (C, D, E, and F). Cutting directions for the bright colors are given per block so that you can easily keep your fabric pieces separated by individual blocks.

From the blue print (A), cut:

- 2 strips, 3⅜" x 42"; crosscut into 15 squares, 3⅜" x 3⅜"

- 7 strips, 2⅞" x 42"; crosscut into 90 squares, 2⅞" x 2⅞"

- 5 border strips, 2" x 42"

- 8 binding strips, 2½" x 42"

From the white print (B), cut:

- 11 strips, 2½" x 42"; crosscut into 60 squares, 2½" x 2½", and 60 rectangles, 2½" x 4½"

- 12 strips, 3" x 42"

- 4 strips, 5¼" x 42"; crosscut into 28 squares, 5¼" x 5¼". Cut each square twice diagonally to yield 112 quarter-square triangles.

- 8 squares, 3¾" x 3¾"; cut each square once diagonally to yield 16 half-square triangles

From the assorted bright prints, cut for *each* block:

- 2 squares, 2⅞" x 2⅞" (C)

- 4 squares, 2⅞" x 2⅞" (D)

- 4 rectangles, 2½" x 4½" (E)

- 2 squares, 2⅞" x 2⅞"; cut each square in half once diagonally to yield 4 triangles (F)

From the remaining bright prints, cut:

- 60 squares, 3⅜" x 3⅜"

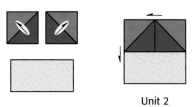

BLOCK CONSTRUCTION

You need 15 blocks for this quilt. Each block uses the same blue (A) and white (B) fabrics. For each block, select a different bright fabric for the C, D, E, and F pieces. Refer to the block diagram below for fabric placement. Lay out the components for each block before piecing them together. Since many of the pieces are the same size, take care to double-check your color placement.

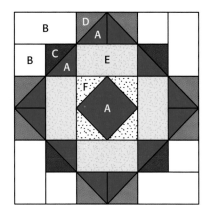

Unit 1

1 Draw a diagonal line on the wrong side of six 2⅞" blue squares and place two of these squares right sides together with the two 2⅞" C squares. (Set aside the remaining blue squares for unit 2.) Sew ¼" away from both sides of the drawn line, and cut the squares apart on the line. Flip the triangles open and press the seam allowance toward fabric C. You'll have four matching triangle squares.

2 Join a white square to the C side of each triangle square to form four rectangles. Then add a white rectangle as shown to complete four units. Press the seam toward B.

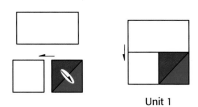

Unit 1

Unit 2

1 Place the remaining four blue squares with diagonal lines right sides together with the four D squares. Sew ¼" away from both sides of the drawn line and cut apart on the line to yield eight triangle squares.

2 Place two of the triangle squares right sides together, blue over blue, and sew them together to form a Flying Geese unit. Make three more identical units, and then sew each unit to a fabric E rectangle. Press the seam toward fabric E.

Unit 2

Unit 3

Sew fabric F triangles to opposite sides of a 3⅜" blue square and press the seams toward the triangles. Add two more F triangles and press in the same manner.

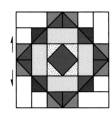

Unit 3

Block Assembly

1 Lay out the units with unit 1 in the corners, unit 3 in the block center, and unit 2 at the top, bottom, and sides. Be sure to orient each piece correctly so that the blue triangles make an on-point square design in the block.

2 Sew the units together into rows and sew the rows together, matching seam intersections. Press the completed block. Repeat to make a total of 15 blocks.

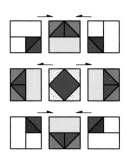

Make 15.

Quilt Assembly

1. Lay out the quilt blocks in five rows of three blocks each, rearranging the blocks until you are happy with the layout.

2. Sew the blocks together into rows, and press the blocks in alternate rows in opposite directions.

3. Sew the rows together and press the quilt top.

Borders

This quilt has a series of four borders: a blue border, a white border, a border of pieced squares, and another white border. This border combination really helps to set off the blocks and make them sparkle on the white background.

First Border

1. Cut one of the 2"-wide blue strips into two equal lengths and sew these half-strips to the ends of full-length strips. Measure the length of the quilt top through the center and trim the two border strips to this measurement, which should be approximately 60½". Sew these blue borders to the sides of the quilt top. Press the seams toward the blue borders.

2. Measure the width of the quilt top through the center and trim the remaining two 2"-wide blue strips to this measurement, which should be approximately 39½". Join the strips to the top and bottom of the quilt top and press the seams toward the blue borders.

Second Border

1. Join five 3"-wide white strips end to end. Cut two borders from this pieced strip to equal the length of the quilt top, which should be approximately 63½". Join the borders to the sides of the quilt top and press the seams toward the blue borders.

2. Measure the width of the quilt top and trim two borders to this measurement, which should be approximately 44½". Join the borders to the top and bottom of the quilt and press the seams toward the blue borders.

Third Border

The side borders are each made up of 17 bright print 3⅜" squares. The top and bottom borders each have 13 squares.

1. Set aside eight of the bright squares for the corner units. Then join white quarter-square triangles to opposite sides of the remaining 52 squares as shown. Press the seams toward the squares.

Make 52.

2. To make the corner units, join two 3¾" white half-square triangles to adjacent sides of the eight bright squares. Then sew one white quarter-square triangle to each of the squares as shown.

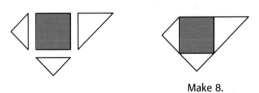

Make 8.

3. For the side borders, sew two strips each with 15 of the units from step 1. Sew a corner unit to each end of these strips. Sew the borders to the sides of the quilt, easing as necessary to fit.

4. For the top and bottom borders, sew two strips each with 11 of the units from step 1. Sew a corner unit to each end of these strips. Sew the borders to the top and bottom of the quilt as for the side borders.

Top or Bottom Border

Side Borders

Fourth Border

❶ Join the seven remaining 3"-wide white strips end to end. From this long strip, cut two borders equal to the length of the quilt top, which should be approximately 76½". Join the borders to opposite sides of the quilt top and press the seams toward the white strips.

❷ Measure the width of the quilt top through the center and cut two borders to this measurement, which should be approximately 57½". Join these strips to the top and bottom of the quilt top. Press as for the side borders.

Quilt Assembly

FINISHING

❶ Cut the backing fabric into two equal lengths and sew the pieces together to make a backing with a vertical seam. Trim the backing so that it is approximately 6" larger than the quilt top.

❷ Layer the quilt top with the batting and backing; baste the layers together.

❸ Hand or machine quilt as desired. Natasha hand quilted her project in the ditch around the block pieces and she quilted heart-shaped flowers in the white areas where the blocks are joined. In the borders, she quilted a diagonal crosshatch design that is the same width as the border squares.

❹ Trim the excess batting and backing fabric even with the edges of the quilt top. Join the blue binding strips with diagonal seams and use them to bind the edges of the quilt.

❺ Label your quilt and attach a hanging sleeve, if desired.

*After making "Happy Hannah" with blue blocks, border, and binding, quiltmaker
Natasha Castelijn made a pink version for her youngest daughter, Laura.
Select your own colorway and dig into that ever-growing scrap pile!*

Finished quilt size: 45" x 59½" (113 cm x 149 cm) • Finished block size: 6" (15.2 cm)

I SPY

"I Spy" quilts are quite popular with children. By using kid-friendly prints, you offer children a fun opportunity to see what they can spy in the quilt blocks. And, with so many juvenile and novelty prints on the market today, it's easy to collect quite a variety of animals, vehicles, insects, or whatever tickles your youngster's fancy. This quilt has plenty of charming prints to look at, so each time children examine the colorful quilt, they're bound to find something new.

In Dorothy Clark's "I Spy" quilt, the blocks are foundation pieced in a lopsided arrangement. When set together, the colorful outer triangles of the blocks form elongated diamonds and a quite intricate-looking setting. The quilt is easier to piece than it looks, making it just as enjoyable for moms to create as it is for kids to look at.

MATERIALS

All yardages are based on 42"-wide (107 cm) fabric unless otherwise noted.

- 61 charm squares, at least 4" x 4" (10 cm square), of novelty prints for block centers
- 4⅛ yards (3.8 m) of black fabric for blocks, borders, and binding
- 3 yards (2.8 m) total of assorted bright solids for blocks
- 3 yards (2.6 m) of backing fabric
- 51" x 66" (130 cm x 168 cm) piece of batting
- 3½ yards (3.2 m) of lightweight, nonfusible interfacing for block foundations*
- Fine-point permanent marker

If your interfacing is only 20"–22" wide, you will need 6½ yards.

CUTTING

All cutting dimensions include ¼" seam allowances.

From the interfacing, cut:

- 61 squares, 7½" x 7½", for block foundations

From the novelty prints, cut:

- 61 squares, 4" x 4"

From the black fabric, cut:

- 35 strips, 3" x 42"; crosscut into 244 rectangles, 3" x 5½"
- 2 strips, 1¾" x 42"; crosscut into 10 rectangles, 1¾" x 6½"
- 8 border strips, 1¾" x 42"
- 6 binding strips, 2¼" x 42"

From the assorted bright solids, cut:

- 61 rectangles, 6½" x 10"

FOUNDATION PREPARATION

The quilt shown contains four different blocks. Block A and block B are mirror images of one another. Blocks D and C are the same as blocks A and B, except that the foundations are rotated 180º for the quilt setting. However, you need to rotate the foundation before sewing so that your novelty prints will appear right side up in the finished quilt.

The A and B foundation patterns are provided on pages 54 and 55. Using a fine-point permanent marker and ruler, trace the patterns to make 16 A foundations and 12 B foundations on the 7½" interfacing squares. Then rotate each pattern 180º (so the writing appears upside down) and trace them to make 18 C foundations and 15 D foundations. Be sure to label each foundation and mark the top of the block so that you will be able to correctly place your directional novelty prints within the blocks.

BLOCK CONSTRUCTION

1. Place a 4" novelty square right side up on the unmarked side of the foundation so that it covers section 1. Hold the foundation and the novelty square up to the light to make sure that the fabric is correctly oriented and that it extends beyond the seam lines. Pin the fabric in place.

2. Place a black 3" x 5½" rectangle on top of the novelty square with right sides together as shown. Hold the foundation up to the light source again to ensure that you have adequate coverage. Pin the black fabric in place.

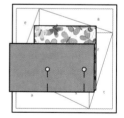

3. Turn the foundation over, so that the sewing-line side is on top, and stitch on the line between sections 1 and 2 using a slightly shorter-than-normal stitch length. Begin and end stitching a few

stitches beyond the ends of the line. Then turn it over to the fabric side and trim the seam allowance to ¼" to reduce bulk as shown. Open the fabric and finger-press the fold flat, then press gently with a cool iron, taking care not to distort the interfacing.

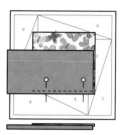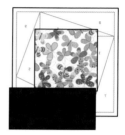

4. Place the next black rectangle into position between sections 1 and 3. Check the seam allowance, and then sew it in place, trim, and press as before. Continue in this manner to complete sections 4 and 5. Repeat these steps for each of the 61 blocks. The remainder of the block piecing is not done until you've decided on your block arrangement for the quilt top.

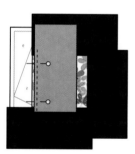

QUILT ASSEMBLY

To form the diamond pattern with the bright solid colors, you will need to decide on your block layout first, and then decide where you want each color to go.

1. Lay out the blocks in seven rows of seven blocks each on your design wall or floor, referring to the layout diagram that follows. Make sure blocks are positioned according to the placement for A, B, C, and D, and that the novelty prints are all facing in the same upright direction.

The top and bottom rows are made only of C and D blocks, and sashing will be added between the blocks to complete these rows. Note that there are only six blocks in each of these rows.

C	D	C	D	C	D

A	B	A	B	A	B	A
C	D	C	D	C	D	C
A	B	A	B	A	B	A
C	D	C	D	C	D	C
A	B	A	B	A	B	A
C	D	C	D	C	D	C
A	B	A	B	A	B	A

C	D	C	D	C	D

2 Once you are happy with their placement, number each block by writing the row and block number in the seam allowance of the interfacing, such as 1-1, 1-2, etc. This will ensure that you sew all the blocks together in the correct order.

3 The diamonds in the design are created when the corners of four adjoining blocks are stitched together. First, cut each of the bright solid rectangles in half horizontally, and then cut each resulting piece in half diagonally to form four triangles.

 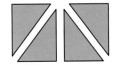

4 Select a set of four matching triangles and place them over the foundations to form a diamond where the color looks appealing. Pin them in place on each foundation. Continue placing the sets of

matching triangles to form diamonds, taking care to distribute the lights and darks evenly across the quilt top. Along the outer edges of rows 2–8, place sets of two bright triangles to create a half-diamond effect.

Use the remaining triangles for the corners and to surround the blocks in the top and bottom rows. *Note:* Using safety pins for the triangles will ensure they stay put until you are ready to stitch them in place.

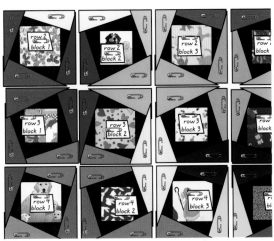

5 One block at a time, take the blocks down from your design wall and sew the bright solid triangles to the four corners of a block in positions 6, 7, 8, and 9. Trim and press as for the black rectangles, and then trim each completed block to 6½". Place the block back in position and continue until you've completed all blocks.

6 Sew a 1¾" x 6½" black sashing strip to the right sides of the first five blocks in the top row. Join these blocks to form a row of six blocks separated by sashing strips. Repeat this process for the blocks in the bottom row.

7 Join the remaining blocks into rows and sew rows 2–8 together. Press. Do not attach the top and bottom rows yet.

Borders

1. Sew five 1¾"-wide black border strips together end to end. From this long strip, cut four borders the same width as your quilt top, which should be approximately 42½". *Note:* If you're lucky enough to have black fabric that is longer than 42", you will not need to piece the strips together. You can simply trim each one to the correct length.

2. Sew a border strip to the top and bottom of the assembled quilt top and press the seams toward the black fabric.

3. Sew row 1 to the top of the quilt and row 9 to the bottom of the quilt, easing as necessary to fit. Make sure the borders are oriented correctly, with the novelty prints upright.

4. Sew the two remaining border strips from step 1 to the top and bottom of the quilt and press the seams toward the black fabric.

5. Join the remaining 1¾"-wide black strips together end to end. Measure the length of the quilt top and cut two side borders from the long strip to this

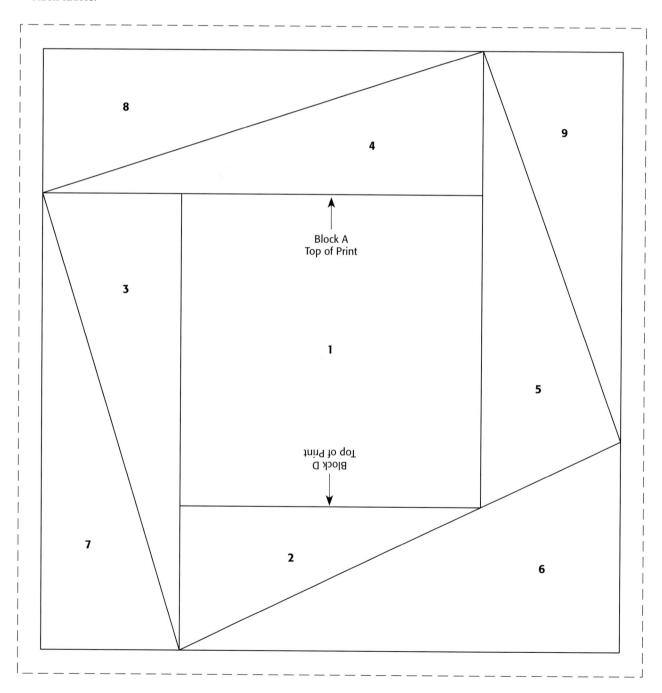

measurement, which should be approximately 59½". Sew the borders to the sides of the quilt top and press the seams toward the black borders.

FINISHING

1 Cut the backing fabric into two equal lengths and sew the pieces together to make a backing with a horizontal seam. Trim the backing so that it is approximately 6" larger than the quilt top.

2 Layer the quilt top with the batting and backing; baste the layers together.

3 Hand or machine quilt as desired. Dorothy's quilt was machine quilted in the ditch around the novelty squares and ¼" inside the edges of the diamonds. In-the-ditch quilting was also used around each block in the top and bottom rows.

4 Trim the excess batting and backing fabric even with the edges of the quilt top. Join the black binding strips with diagonal seams and use them to bind the edges of the quilt.

5 Label your quilt and attach a hanging sleeve, if desired.

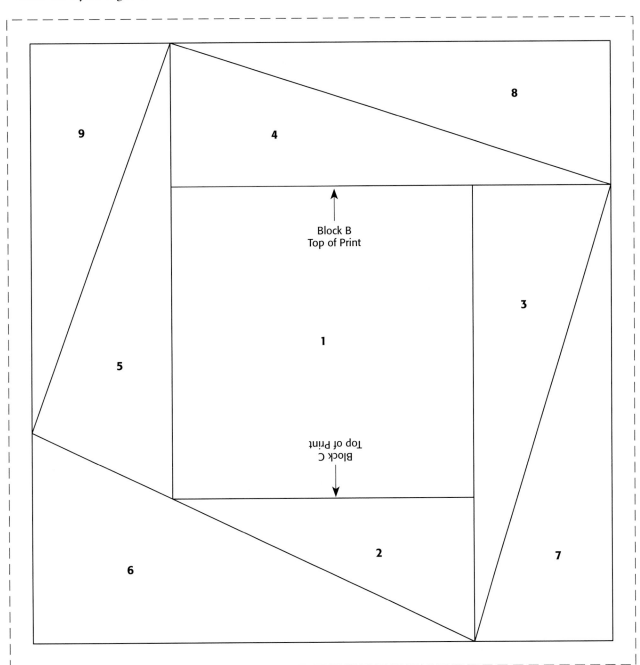

Finished quilt size: 65" x 70" (165 cm x 178 cm)
Finished block sizes: Cross block: 5" (13 cm); Ohio Star block: 6" (15 cm)

FIVE-PATCH CROSS

Joy White made this quilt simply because she loves the color combination—
and that is all the reason one should need! Joy chose orange, purple, and
green—all secondary colors spaced equally apart on the color wheel. Because there's
quite a bit of contrast between the colors, it's best to use more of one and less of
another so they don't end up battling for attention. That's just what Joy has done.
Her quilt is mostly orange with a hearty dose of green. The cool purples are used
more sparingly and provide a place for your eyes to rest.

MATERIALS

*All yardages are based on 42"-wide (107 cm) fabric unless
otherwise noted.*

- ⅓ yard (30 cm) *each* of 15 assorted orange and gold
  prints for blocks and Ohio Star border

- 12 to 15 fat quarters of assorted greens, tans, dark
  reds, and purples for blocks and checkerboard border

- 1 yard (90 cm) of olive green print for triangle and
  outer borders

- 1 yard (90 cm) of black print for triangle and outer
  borders

- ⅓ yard (30 cm) of gold print for middle border

- ½ yard (50 cm) of brown print for binding

- 4¼ yards (3.9 m) of backing fabric

- 71" x 76" (175 cm x 188 cm) piece of batting

Create Your Own Colorway

The vivid colors in this quilt look very striking,
but a more subdued palette could be equally
pleasing. Why not experiment with your own
color combinations?

Because of the scrappy nature of the quilt,
each block looks slightly different, with varied
color placement giving added interest to the
quilt design.

CUTTING

All cutting dimensions include ¼" seam allowances.

From the assorted orange and gold prints, cut a total of:

- 20 rectangles, ranging in size from 4" x 6½" to 8½" x 6½"; all rectangles must be 6½" wide

From the assorted fat quarters and the remaining orange and gold prints, cut:

- For Cross blocks:
    - 224 squares, 2½" x 2½"
    - 224 rectangles, 1½" x 2½"
    - 56 squares, 1½" x 1½"
- For checkerboard border:
    - 128 rectangles, 1¾" x 2"
    - 136 squares, 2" x 2"
- For Ohio Star blocks:
    - 100 squares, 2½" x 2½"
    - 80 squares, 3¼" x 3¼"

From the black print, cut:

- 2 strips, 6⅜" x 42"; crosscut into 8 squares, 6⅜" x 6⅜". Cut each square twice diagonally to yield 32 triangles (2 will be extra).
- 8 border strips, 1½" x 42"

From the olive green print, cut:

- 2 strips, 6⅜" x 42"; crosscut into 7 squares, 6⅜" x 6⅜". Cut each square twice diagonally to yield 28 triangles (2 will be extra).
- 2 squares, 5⅞" x 5⅞"; cut each square once diagonally to yield 4 triangles
- 8 border strips, 1½" x 42"

From the light orange print, cut:

- 6 border strips, 1¾" x 42"

From the brown print, cut:

- 7 binding strips, 2¼" x 42"

CROSS BLOCK ASSEMBLY

You need 56 Cross blocks for this quilt. Each block uses a different combination of fabrics. For each block you will need four matching 2½" squares, four matching 1½" x 2½" rectangles, and one 1½" square.

❶ Lay out the pieces for one block at a time, referring to the illustration. Stitch the pieces together into rows and then stitch the rows together. Repeat to make 56 blocks. You may choose to wait to do final pressing until you have arranged your blocks so that you can press adjoining seams in opposite directions.

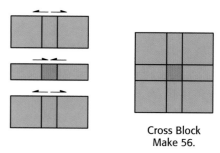

Cross Block
Make 56.

❷ Lay out the blocks in eight rows of seven blocks each. Rearrange them until you are happy with your color placements. Join the blocks into rows, pressing the seams on the odd-numbered rows to the right and those on the even-numbered rows to the left.

❸ Sew the rows together to form the central section of the quilt top, carefully butting the seam intersection. Press.

BORDERS

This quilt has a series of five borders. The first is pieced from black and green triangles, the second is a checkerboard design, the third is a plain orange border, the fourth is pieced from Ohio Star blocks and plain rectangles, and the final border is strip pieced from green and black strips.

Triangle Border

❶ Join the triangles into two strips of seven black and six olive green triangles for the top and bottom of the quilt, and two strips of eight black and seven olive green triangles for the side borders. Make

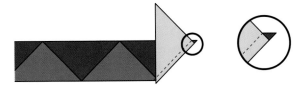

sure you offset the points where the stitching begins so that your border edges will be even. Press the seams toward the black triangles.

Top or Bottom Border
Make 2.

Side Border
Make 2.

2 With the black triangles adjacent to the quilt top, stitch the longer strips to the sides of the quilt top and the shorter strips to the top and bottom. Press the seams toward the borders.

3 Add the four large olive green corner triangles to complete the border.

Checkerboard Border

1 Stitch the assorted 1¾" x 2" rectangles into pairs, sewing along the short ends. Press the seams to one side.

2 Sew the pairs together side by side along the long edges to create two borders, each 32 units long. The borders should measure 40½" long. Sew the completed border strips to the top and bottom of the quilt top, easing if necessary to fit. Press the seams toward the triangle borders.

1¾"

3 Stitch the assorted 2" squares together into pairs. Stitch the pairs together side by side along the long edges to create two borders, each 34 units long. The borders should measure 51½" long. Sew them to opposite sides of the quilt top, matching seams where they join the top and bottom borders. Press the seams toward the triangle borders.

Orange Border

1 Join the six light orange border strips end to end into one long length using diagonal seams. Press the seams open. From the long strip, cut two side borders 51½" long and top and bottom borders 49" long.

2 Stitch the longer strips to the sides of the quilt top. Press the seams toward the yellow border. Add the shorter strips to the top and bottom of the quilt and press as for the side borders.

Ohio Star Border

You need 20 Ohio Star blocks for the border, in addition to the assorted orange rectangles and squares. For each Ohio Star block you will need four 2½" squares and two 3¼" squares from a main color, and one 2½" square and two 3¼" squares from a contrasting color.

1 Using a pencil, draw a diagonal line from corner to corner across the wrong side of each of the large contrasting squares. Place these squares on top of the large main-color squares, right sides together. Stitch ¼" away from each side of the drawn line. Cut the squares apart on the line and press open the resulting four triangle squares, with the seams toward the darker fabric.

2 Draw a diagonal line across the triangle squares, from the main color to the contrasting color, on the wrong side of two of the triangle squares as shown. Pair the triangle squares right sides together, butting the seams, and with the two different colors facing one another. The triangle squares with the pencil lines should be on top.

Stitch ¼" away from each side of the drawn line as before. Cut on the pencil line and press the quarter-square-triangle units open.

3 Stitch the plain squares and quarter-square-triangle units together into three rows, and stitch the rows together to make an Ohio Star block. Repeat to make 20 blocks.

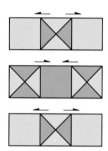 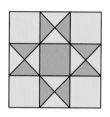

Ohio Star Block
Make 20.

4 Measure the length and width of your quilt top. For the top and bottom borders, alternate five assorted orange rectangles and four Ohio Star blocks, and sew them together. Press the seams toward the orange rectangles. Trim the borders to fit the width of your quilt, which should be about 49". Sew the borders to the top and bottom of the quilt. Press the seams toward the orange borders.

Top or Bottom Border
Make 2.

5 For the side borders, sew together five assorted orange pieces and four Ohio Star blocks. These borders need to be a bit longer, so use some of the larger rectangles for these borders. Press the seams

toward the orange rectangles. Trim the borders to the length of your quilt top, not including the top and bottom borders you added in the preceding step. This measurement should be approximately 54". Then add the remaining four Ohio Star blocks to the ends of the border strips. Join the borders to the sides of the quilt. Press the seams toward the orange borders.

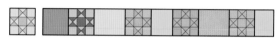

Side Border
Make 2.

Outer Border

1 Join the black border strips end to end in pairs to make four long strips. Do the same with the olive green border strips. Then sew the black and green strips together along the long edges to make four long border strips. Press the seams toward the black fabric.

Make 4.

2 The outer border is added to the quilt Log Cabin style, starting with the bottom border. Trim one of the long strips to the width of the quilt. Sew this border to the bottom of the quilt with the black strip adjoining the Ohio Star border. Press the seam toward the black border.

3 Measure the length of your quilt, including the bottom border. Trim one of the long border strips to this length and sew it to the left side of the quilt in the same manner as for the bottom border. Continue around the quilt, next trimming and sewing a border to fit the top of your quilt and finally one for the right side of the quilt, referring to the quilt assembly diagram opposite.

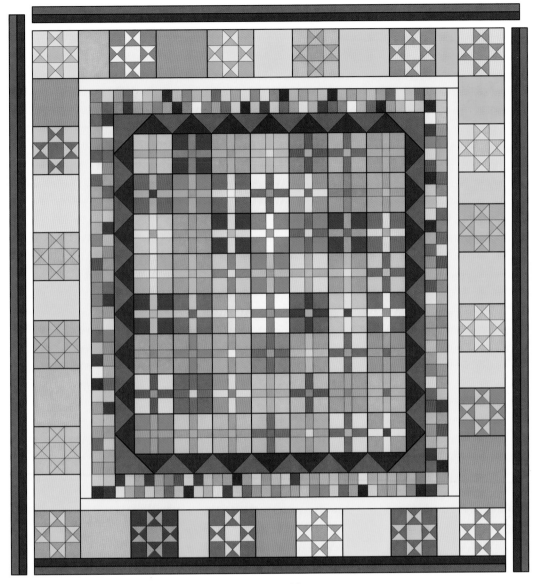

Quilt Assembly

FINISHING

1 Cut the backing fabric into two equal lengths and sew the pieces together to make a backing with a horizontal seam. Trim the backing so that it is approximately 6" larger than the quilt top.

2 Layer the quilt top with the batting and backing; baste the layers together.

3 Hand or machine quilt as desired. Joy hand quilted both the Cross blocks and the Ohio Star blocks in the ditch. The triangles in the first border are

quilted ½" inside the triangle edges. The checkerboard border is quilted diagonally to create a zigzag pattern. The spacing rectangles in the Ohio Star border are quilted in parallel lines 1" apart.

4 Trim the excess batting and backing fabric even with the edges of the quilt top. Join the brown print binding strips with diagonal seams and use them to bind the edges of the quilt.

5 Label your quilt and attach a hanging sleeve, if desired.

Finished quilt size: 72½" x 72½" (184 cm square) • Finished block size: 12" (30 cm)

FRIENDSHIP SPOOLS

If your scrap bag is lacking bits of brightly colored fabrics, you can do what quiltmaker Judy Hansen did. Ask your quilting friends to help you out! Judy provided the black fabric for continuity, and then she enlisted the help of the St. Ives Quilters to make the Spool blocks for her quilt. The colors and patterns really pop off the black background, and the shocking pink border adds some extra punch.

MATERIALS

All yardages are based on 42"-wide (107 cm) fabric unless otherwise noted.

- 3¼ yards (2.9 m) of black solid for block backgrounds and Flying Geese border
- 3¼ yards (2.9 m) total of assorted bright prints for spool ends (The 2 ends of one spool can be cut from an 8" [20 cm] square.)
- 1¾ yards (1.6 m) of pink mottled fabric for outer border
- ½ yard (40 cm) total of assorted stripes and other print scraps for spool centers
- ⅓ yard (30 cm) *each* of 6 bright tone-on-tone prints for Flying Geese border
- ⅓ yard (30 cm) of yellow print for inner border
- ¼ yard (20 cm) of blue print for inner border
- ⅞ yard (80 cm) of blue print for binding
- 4⅔ yards (4.3 m) of backing fabric
- 78" x 78" (200 cm square) piece of batting
- Template plastic
- Fine-point permanent marker
- White pencil for marking fabric
- Foundation paper for Flying Geese border

CUTTING

All cutting dimensions include ¼" seam allowances. The patterns for A and B spool pieces are on page 66.

From the black solid, cut:

- 11 strips, 4" x 42"; crosscut into 136 rectangles, 3" x 4", and 4 squares, 4" x 4"
- 136 A pieces

From the assorted bright prints for spools, cut:

- 68 matching pairs of A pieces

From the assorted stripes and other scraps, cut:

- 68 B pieces

From the yellow print, cut:

- 4 strips, 2" x 42"; crosscut into 8 strips, 2" x 18½"

From the blue print, cut:

- 2 strips, 2" x 42"; crosscut into 4 strips, 2" x 12½", and 4 squares, 2" x 2"

From *each* of the 6 bright tone-on-tone prints, cut:

- 2 strips, 4½" x 42"; crosscut into 24 rectangles, 3" x 4½" (144 total)

From the pink mottled fabric, cut lengthwise:

- 4 border strips, 6½" x length of fabric

From the blue binding fabric, cut:

- 8 strips, 3½" x 42"

BLOCK CONSTRUCTION

This quilt is made of sixteen 12" blocks, each made from four 6" spools. Four spools are needed for the border corners, so you need 68 spools in all.

1 Make plastic templates of the A and B patterns on page 66. Copy the grain line markings and all other details from the patterns. Use the patterns to trace and then cut out the number of pieces as described in the list of cutting instructions.

2 Stitch a bright print A to a contrasting B square, starting and stopping ¼" from each side of the square to leave the seam allowance free.

3 Join a black A to the print A, beginning ¼" from the inner corner where they meet the square and sewing all the way to the outer corner. Then join the seam of the black A and the B square. Add the second bright print A and then the second black A in the same manner.

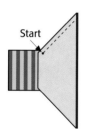

Start

4 Repeat to make 68 spools. Set four of them aside for the outer border corners, and join the rest together in sets of four, alternating the direction of the spools as shown, to make 16 large blocks.

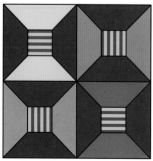

Large Spool Block
Make 16.

Small Spool Block
Make 4.

QUILT ASSEMBLY

1 Referring to the quilt photograph on page 62, arrange the blocks in four rows of four blocks each. Rearrange them until you are satisfied with the color placement. Be sure that the black backgrounds adjoin the colored spool ends throughout the quilt top.

2 Sew the blocks together into rows, and then sew the rows together. Press the quilt top.

INNER BORDER

1 Measure the width and length of the quilt top through the center. It should measure 48½" x 48½". Join a 2" x 18½" yellow strip to either end of the four 2" x 12½" blue strips and press. Your completed strips should also measure 48½" long. However, if necessary, trim these strips to fit your quilt top.

Inner Border
Make 4.

2 Matching the ends of the blue strips with the edges of the two center spools, join the border strips to opposite sides of the quilt top. Press the seams toward the borders.

3 Sew a 2" blue square to each end of the two remaining border strips. Press the seams toward the yellow fabric. Then join these borders to the top and bottom of the quilt top, matching the center seams as before. Press the seam allowances toward the borders.

FLYING GEESE BORDER

1 Make 24 copies of the Flying Geese border foundation pattern on page 67. You can either trace the pattern onto lightweight paper or interfacing, or photocopy it. Each side of the quilt has 34 individual Flying Geese in it, so you need six border foundations for each side of the quilt. That will give you 36 geese per border, or two extra. On one foundation pattern per side of the quilt you will need to cut off two of the geese units. Remember

to allow for seam allowance on the end of the foundation where you trim off two geese. Copy four corner foundations from page 67 also.

2 The Flying Geese borders are pieced using the rectangles of black and six different bright tone-on-tone print fabrics. To make piecing easier, cut the bright rectangles in half so you have matching pieces 2¼" x 3".

3 To evenly distribute your bright colors around the quilt, piece each foundation using each bright color for one geese unit. All the large center triangles are pieced from the black solid. With the marked side of the foundation facing up, place one rectangle of black fabric under area 1. Place the bright print fabric right sides together with the black fabric so that it covers areas 1 and 2 and pin in place along the stitching line. Flip the bright fabric back to make sure that when it's sewn it will cover all of area 2, plus the seam allowances. If it does not, remove the pin and adjust the placement until it does.

From the paper side, stitch along the marked line between areas 1 and 2, sewing a few stitches beyond each end of the line to secure the pieces.

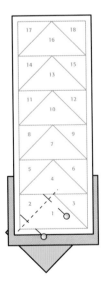

4 Double-check to make sure the bright fabric completely covers area 2 and the seam allowances. Then trim away the excess fabric, leaving a ¼" seam allowance. Flip open the bright fabric and press.

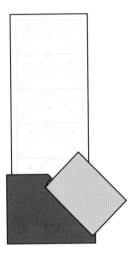

5 Add the matching 2¼" x 3" bright rectangle to cover area 3 of the foundation in the same manner.

6 Continue adding fabrics, in numerical order, until the entire foundation piece is covered. Remember, the black fabric is always used for the large center triangles, and matching bright fabrics are used on either side of it to cover the small triangles.

When the entire foundation is covered, press the unit and use your rotary cutter and ruler to trim off the excess fabric. Do not trim away the marked seam allowances.

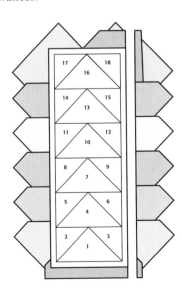

7 Foundation piece the four border corner squares in the same manner, using the 4" black solid squares for the centers of the blocks, and two sets of matching bright print pieces for each block, as shown.

Corner
Make 4.

8 For each side of the quilt, sew together six foundations, making sure all the geese are pointing in the same direction. Remember, you need five complete border sections (six geese each) and one with only four geese per border.

9 Sew a Flying Geese border to the right side of the quilt top with the black triangles pointing downward. Sew another border to the left side of the quilt with the black triangles pointing upward.

10 Sew a corner square to each end of the remaining two borders. Then sew the borders to the quilt so that the black triangles in the top border point toward the right and the triangles in the bottom border point toward the left. Do not remove the paper foundations at this stage.

OUTER BORDER

1 Measure the width and length of your quilt top. It should be 57½" x 57½". Trim all four pink mottled border strips to this length.

2 Sew a pink border to the left and right sides of the quilt. Press the seams toward the pink fabric.

3 Sew the four Spool blocks set aside from "Block Construction" on page 64 to the ends of the two remaining pink border strips. Press the seams toward the pink fabric. Then sew the borders to the top and bottom of the quilt. Press the seams toward the pink borders.

4 Carefully remove the papers from the Flying Geese border and press the quilt top.

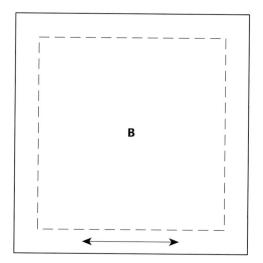

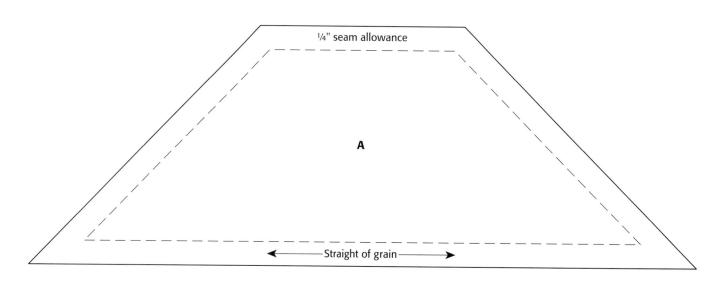

FINISHING

1. Cut the backing fabric into two equal lengths and sew the pieces together to make a backing with a vertical seam. Trim the backing so that it is approximately 6" larger than the quilt top.

2. Layer the quilt top with the batting and backing; baste the layers together.

3. Hand or machine quilt as desired. Judy hand quilted with black thread on the print fabrics and with blue thread on the black background areas. She quilted ¼" inside each A piece, using ¼" masking tape as a guide. The squares in the center of each spool were quilted with parallel lines ¼" apart to represent threads.

   The inner border was quilted in a zigzag pattern to form triangles. The two short sides of the black Flying Geese triangles were outline quilted ¼" inside the edges, and the wide outer border was quilted with spool shapes that were traced onto the border with templates.

4. For binding, Judy used a wide, single-fold binding, and she left 1" worth of batting and backing fabric in place to fill out the binding. You may do the same, or you might choose a more traditional double-fold binding. See "Binding" on page 94 for more details.

5. Label your quilt and attach a hanging sleeve, if desired.

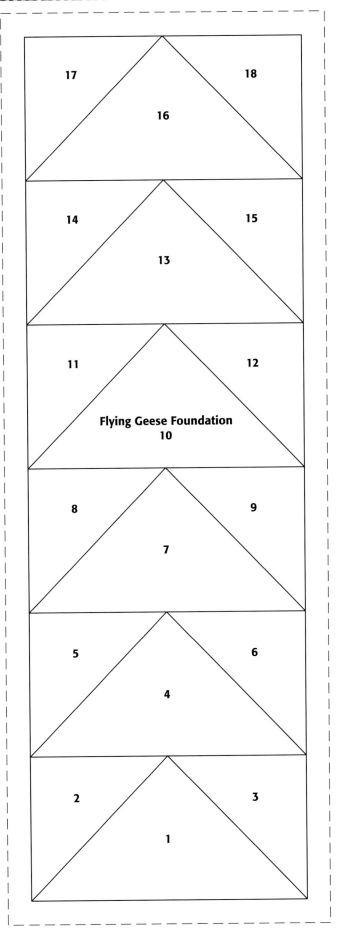

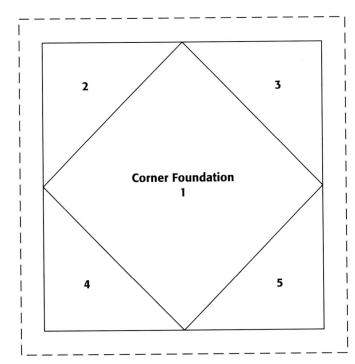

Finished quilt size: 91" x 91" (231 cm square) • Finished block size: 7" (17.75 cm)

SQUARE DANCE

Kimberly Barrett made this riot-of-color quilt using a wide variety of bright hand-dyed fabrics, stitching them together in an endless array of color combinations. This quilt is a celebration of color and was a journey of discovery for Kimberly. She found each new color combination seemed to suggest yet another option. The instructions are based on using fat eighths of each fabric, although you could substitute smaller pieces of fabrics if you want to incorporate even more colors in your quilt.

MATERIALS

All yardages are based on 42"-wide (107 cm) fabric unless otherwise noted.

- 72 fat eighths of bright hand-dyed fabrics in a wide variety of colors including yellow, red, blue, rust, brown, burgundy, purple, blue, teal, orange, olive, lime green, and hot pink for blocks. Tonal values should include approximately:

  - 10 dark
  - 18 medium-dark
  - 24 medium
  - 12 medium-light
  - 8 light

- 12 fat quarters in a similar range of bright colors and tones for border and binding
- 8½ yards (7.7 m) of backing fabric
- 97" x 97" (244 cm square) piece of batting
- Template plastic

Note: If using scraps, you'll need a total of 14 yards (13 m), made up of pieces measuring at least 9" (23 cm) square, or 180 strips measuring 5" x 18" (13 cm x 46 cm) for the blocks, border, and binding.

CUTTING

All cutting dimensions include ¼" seam allowances. The border triangle pattern is on page 73.

From *each* of the bright fat eighths, cut:

- 2 strips, 4½" x 9"; from each strip cut 1 square, 4½" x 4½", and 2 strips, 2" x 4½"
- 1 strip, 7½" x 9"; crosscut into 2 strips, 2" x 7½"

Note: As you cut the pieces from each color, stack them into sets consisting of 1 square, 2 long strips, and 2 short strips. This is a single color set. Keep the sets separated.

From *each* of the bright fat quarters, cut:

- 3 strips, 4½" x 18" (36 total) (Be sure to cut parallel to the selvage edge and not crosswise, or you won't have enough fabric left to cut binding strips.)
- 2 binding strips, 2½" x 18"

BLOCK CONSTRUCTION

You need 144 blocks for this quilt. The blocks are sewn as pairs, reversing the position of the two fabrics from one block to the other in each pair. When combining the pairs of fabric, vary the tonal contrasts as well as the color combinations. In the quilt shown, 8 sets have light colors with low tonal contrast, 12 sets have dark colors with low tonal contrast, 12 sets have high contrast, and 40 sets have medium contrast using dark, medium, and light tones. Using the quilt photograph on page 68 as a guide, make 72 two-color sets using the following directions and taking care not to repeat a combination.

❶ Lay out the pieces for two blocks, placing the large square of each color in the block centers. Place the short strips of the contrasting color on opposite sides of each center square, and the long strips of the contrasting color at the top and bottom of the block.

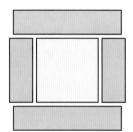 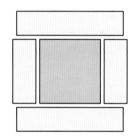

❷ Stitch the short strips to the opposite sides of the square and press the seams toward the strips. Stitch the long strips to the top and bottom, and press the seams toward the strips. Repeat for the second block in the pair and pin it to the first block to keep the pair together.

❸ Repeat steps 1 and 2 to make all 144 blocks.

QUILT ASSEMBLY

❶ Using the floor or a design wall, lay out the blocks in 12 rows of 12 blocks each, keeping the pairs together. Vary the placement so that some pairs are horizontal and others are vertical, referring to the quilt photograph for suggestions. This use of adjoining pairs strengthens the reverse color effect and increases the subtle illusion created by the positive/negative color placement.

❷ When you are satisfied with the color placement throughout your quilt top, unpin the pairs of blocks and rotate the blocks (keeping them in the same position within the quilt) so that the long strips of one block will be joined to the short strips of the next block. This will prevent the need to match any seams other than those of the block rows. It will also help to reduce bulk.

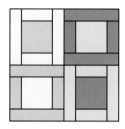

❸ Sew the blocks together into rows and press the seams toward the long strips. Stitch the rows together and press the quilt top.

BORDER

❶ Make a plastic template of the border triangle pattern on page 73. The pattern includes ¼" seam allowances.

❷ Use the template to cut seven border triangles from each of the 4½"-wide strips cut from the bright fat quarters. You'll have 252 triangles; only 244 are needed. The extra triangles will give you more variety as you plan your color placement.

To cut the triangles, place the template on the strips as shown so that the bottom of the triangle is along the cut edge of the strip. You can mark the cutting lines on either side of the template, or simply place your ruler on top of the positioned template and cut along the edge of the ruler. Reposition the template and continue cutting.

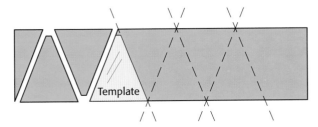

Template

3 In the quilt shown, the triangles are stitched together in color sets of three or four triangles. The corners of the border are mitered, so plan to have a color set flow around each corner. Place the quilt top on the floor or on your design wall and arrange the colors for the border, placing the lighter-toned triangles along the outer edge and the darker triangles butting the interior of the quilt. Rearrange the triangles until you are satisfied with the color placement.

4 The triangles are stitched in pairs, and then the pairs are stitched together. Be sure to offset the points of the triangles as you stitch them so that the finished border will have even edges.

5 Complete one border by sewing a total of 61 triangles together, and press the seam allowances in one direction, taking care not to stretch the border. Measure the outer edge of the border; it should be

at least 93" long to allow for the miter. If necessary, you can add two extra triangles to one end of the border. Make the remaining borders the same length.

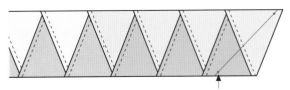

6 Measure the width and length of your quilt top. It should measure approximately 84½" square. Check to make sure that the center and outer-edge measurements are the same. If necessary, make adjustments in the seam lines now to correct the difference so that the pieced border will fit properly.

7 Deduct ½" from your quilt measurement (84") and divide that measurement in half (42"). Find the midpoint of one border strip and mark it with a pin on the inner edge (the dark triangle side). Lay the border on a flat surface and measure away from the midpoint the same distance as your half-quilt measurement (42"). Place a pin at this mark and repeat this procedure for the other end of the border.

Repeat the measuring and pin marking for the other three borders. It is important for the pin marks to be in exactly the same position on the end triangles of the border sections to ensure that each mitered corner will align.

8 Mark a pencil dot at the pin marks, ¼" away from the edge of the border, on the wrong side of the fabric. Repeat this on all corners. Draw a line through the dots at a 45° angle to the long edge of the border. This is the stitching line for the miter.

Mark stitching line.

71

9 Pin mark the midpoints on the outer edges of the quilt top and pin mark each corner ¼" from the edge. Pin the border to the quilt top, matching the pins.

10 Stitch the first border to the quilt top, beginning ¼" from the edge, as marked. Begin and end your stitching with about ¼" of backstitching to secure the seams. Repeat for all borders.

11 To stitch the miter, with the right sides of the borders together, place a pin through the dots on the borders. Then pin along the pencil line, checking to make sure that the drawn line on the underneath border is also aligned with the pins. Stitch along the pencil line from the outer edge to the corner of the quilt top; stop at the dot and secure with backstitching. Double-check to be sure that the seams are aligned and that the corners lie flat before cutting away the excess border fabric. Trim, leaving a ¼" seam allowance. Press the corner seams open and the border seam allowances toward the center.

FINISHING

1 Cut the backing fabric into three equal lengths and sew the pieces together to make a backing with two vertical seams. Trim the backing so that it is approximately 6" larger than the quilt top.

2 Layer the quilt top with the batting and backing; baste the layers together.

3 Hand or machine quilt as desired. Kimberly's quilt was freehand machine quilted in a continuous paisley pattern, using different-colored threads. The strong geometric pattern lends itself to curved stitching. Another effective option would be the Baptist Fan pattern, quilted by hand using pearl cotton and big stitches.

4 Trim the excess batting and backing fabric even with the edges of the quilt top. Join the bright binding strips with diagonal seams and use them to bind the edges of the quilt.

5 Label your quilt and attach a hanging sleeve, if desired.

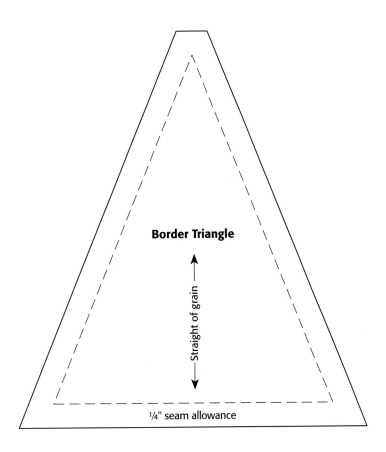

Border Triangle

Straight of grain

¼" seam allowance

Finished quilt size: 49" x 49" (124 cm square) • Finished block size: 4½" (11.5 cm)

AMISH NINE PATCH

True to the Amish belief that only God can make something perfect,
Margie May included a "mistake" in her charming rendition of a popular Amish quilt
design. Amish quilts are frequently characterized by their use of solid fabrics, which
were often scraps left over from other projects or the usable parts of old clothing.
Whether you use fabrics from your scrap bag or purchase new ones,
you'll find this delightful little quilt is quick and easy to stitch.

MATERIALS

All yardages are based on 42"-wide (107 cm) fabric unless otherwise noted.

- 1½ yards (1.3 m) of navy blue solid for outer border
- ¾ yard (70 cm) of dark pink solid for setting squares and triangles
- ⅝ yard (60 cm) of chartreuse solid for inner border
- ½ yard (40 cm) total of assorted light, medium, and dark blue solids for Nine Patch blocks
- ¼ yard (20 cm) *each* of gold and red solids for Nine Patch blocks
- ⅝ yard (60 cm) of black solid for binding
- 3½ yards (3 m) of backing fabric
- 55" x 55" (150 cm square) piece of batting

CUTTING

All cutting dimensions include ¼" seam allowances.

From the medium and dark blue solids, cut:

- 14 sets of 5 squares, 2" x 2" (70 total)
- 2 sets of 4 squares, 2" x 2" (8 total)

From the light blue solid, cut:

- 2 sets of 5 squares, 2" x 2" (10 total)

From the red solids, cut:

- 6 sets of 4 squares, 2" x 2" (24 total)
- 1 square, 2" x 2"

From the gold solids, cut:

- 7 sets of 4 squares, 2" x 2" (28 total)
- 1 set of 3 squares, 2" x 2"

From the dark pink solid, cut:

- 2 strips, 5" x 42"; crosscut into 9 squares, 5" x 5"
- 1 strip, 8⅜" x 42"; crosscut into 3 squares, 8⅜" x 8⅜". Cut each square twice diagonally to yield 12 setting triangles.

(continued on page 76)

Cutting (continued from page 75)

- 2 squares, 5¼" x 5¼"; cut each square once diagonally to yield 4 corner triangles

From the chartreuse solid, cut:

- 4 border strips, 5" x 42"

From the navy blue solid, cut on the lengthwise grain:

- 4 border strips, 6¾" x length of fabric

From the black solid, cut:

- 6 binding strips, 3" x 42"

BLOCK CONSTRUCTION

You need 16 Nine Patch blocks for this quilt. In the quilt shown, all the blocks use either medium or dark blue combined with another color. Seven blocks use gold squares, six blocks use red squares, and two blocks use light blue. One block combines red and gold along with the blue squares to deliberately create an "imperfect" block.

1. Select a set of five dark blue squares and four red squares. Lay them out as shown.

2. Join the three squares in each row and press all seams toward the blue squares. Join the rows to complete the block. Repeat to make six blocks with red squares.

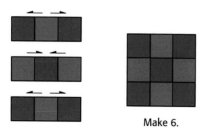

Make 6.

3. Repeat steps 1 and 2 to make seven blocks with gold and blue squares.

Make 7.

4. Make the two blue blocks by laying out five light blue squares and four dark blue squares. Sew the block as described in the preceding steps.

Make 2.

5. To make the single renegade, or imperfect, block, lay out five dark blue squares, three gold squares, and one red square as shown. Sew the block together in the same manner as the other blocks.

Make 1.

QUILT ASSEMBLY

1. Lay out the blocks in four rows of four blocks each, turning the blocks so they are on point. Place the dark pink squares between the rows of Nine Patch blocks. Finally, lay the setting triangles and corner triangles around the perimeter to complete the quilt layout. Rearrange the blocks until you are satisfied with your color placement.

2 Referring to the quilt assembly diagram, opposite, sew the blocks and setting triangles together in diagonal rows. (Note that the pink setting triangles are slightly oversized to create the effect that the Nine Patch blocks are "floating" on the pink background.) Press the seams toward the dark pink squares. Sew the rows together, butting the seams at the intersections.

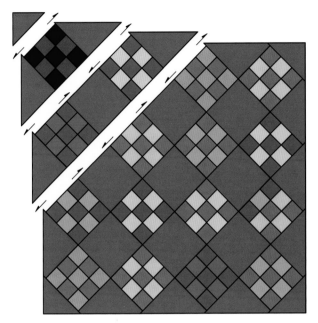

Quilt Assembly

3 Use a rotary cutter and ruler to trim the center of the quilt to 27½" square. Take care not to stretch the edges of the setting triangles.

BORDERS

1 Measure the length of the quilt through the center and trim two of the chartreuse border strips to this length, which should be 27½". Attach the borders to the sides of the quilt top and press the seams toward the borders.

2 Measure the width of the quilt and trim the remaining two chartreuse border strips to this length, which should be 36½". Attach the borders to the top and bottom of the quilt top and press the seams toward the borders.

3 The outer navy blue border is attached in the same manner as the chartreuse border. Measure the length of the quilt top and trim two of the navy blue borders to this length (36½") for the sides of the quilt. After attaching these side borders, measure the quilt width and trim the remaining two border strips to this length (49"). Attach these strips to the top and bottom of your quilt, and press the seams toward the navy blue borders.

FINISHING

1 Cut the backing fabric into two equal lengths and sew the pieces together to make a backing with a vertical seam. Trim the backing so that it is approximately 6" larger than the quilt top.

2 Layer the quilt top with the batting and backing; baste the layers together.

3 Hand or machine quilt as desired. Margie's quilt was hand quilted using brown quilting thread. She quilted straight lines diagonally through each square in the Nine Patch blocks, and a traditional Amish pattern, the pumpkin seed, on both borders. You can make a 4"-diameter circle to mark your own pumpkin seed design, if desired.

4 Trim the excess batting and backing fabric even with the edges of the quilt top. Join the black binding strips with diagonal seams and use them to bind the edges of the quilt.

5 Label your quilt and attach a hanging sleeve, if desired.

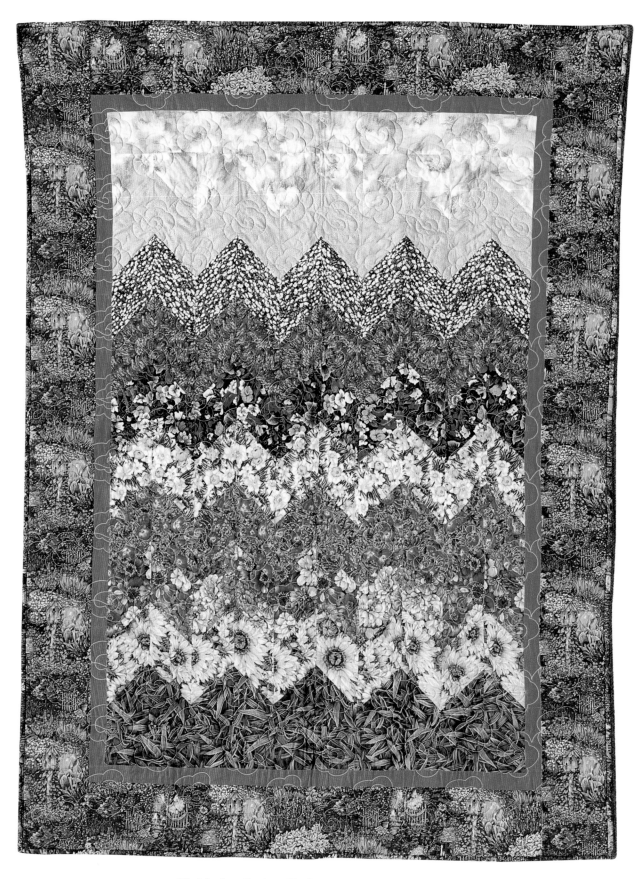

Finished quilt size: 50½" x 66½" (125 cm x 159 cm)

GARDEN GATE

Rosemary Walker designed this bright and beautiful quilt in celebration of the blooms of spring. It's assembled using an easy Seminole-piecing technique. Because the entire quilt center is made using strip sets and segments cut from them, you can easily make this quilt in a day or a weekend. The stunning result is reminiscent of a field of flowers viewed from the garden gate of a mountain chalet.

MATERIALS

All yardages are based on 42"-wide (107 cm) fabric unless otherwise noted.

- ½ yard (40 cm) of a green leaf print for patchwork
- ½ yard (40 cm) of a blue cloud print for patchwork
- ⅓ yard (30 cm) of blue tone-on-tone print for patchwork
- ⅓ yard (30 cm) *each* of 7 different floral prints for patchwork
- ⅓ yard (30 cm) of pink solid for inner border
- 2¼ yards (2 m) of a garden print for outer border and binding
- 3⅓ yards (3 m) of backing fabric
- 54" x 65" (137 cm x 165 cm) piece of batting

CUTTING

All cutting dimensions include ¼" seam allowances.

From the blue cloud print, cut:
- 2 strips, 4" x 42"
- 1 strip, 4½" x 42"

From the green leaf print, cut:
- 2 strips, 4" x 42"
- 1 strip, 4½" x 42"

From *each* of the 7 floral prints, cut:
- 2 strips, 4" x 42"

From the blue tone-on-tone print, cut:
- 2 strips, 4" x 42"

From the pink solid, cut:
- 5 strips, 2" x 42"

From the garden print, cut:
- 2 border strips, 6½" x 42"

From the remaining garden print, cut on the lengthwise grain:
- 2 border strips, 6½" x length of fabric
- 4 binding strips, 2½" x length of fabric

QUILT ASSEMBLY

1 Divide the 4"-wide floral prints, blue prints, and leaf print strips into two groups, with one strip of each fabric in each group. Referring to the quilt photograph on page 78 as a guide, lay out the strips in the same order in each group.

2 Working with the first set of strips, divide the group into two sets of five strips. The first group should contain the green leaf print and the first four floral prints in the order you want them to appear in your quilt. The second group should contain the next three floral prints, followed by the blue tone-on-tone print and the blue cloud print.

Sew the first group of strips together along their long edges, offsetting the end of each fabric 4" to the left, as shown. Press all the seams toward the green leaf print. Repeat for the second group of strips, again offsetting the ends by 4" and pressing the seams away from the sky fabrics.

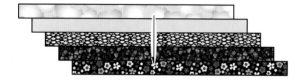

3 Working with the second set of strips, divide them as you did with the first set. Sew the strips together along their long edges, offsetting the end of each fabric 4" to the right, as shown. Press all seams away from the green leaf print and toward the sky fabrics.

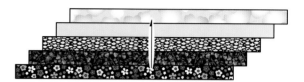

4 Align the 45° line on your ruler with one of the seams in the strip set so that the edge of the ruler is angled along the stair-step edge of the strip set. Cut off the ragged ends. Slide the ruler over so that the 45° line is still aligned with one of the seam lines and the edge of the ruler is 4" from the angled cut edge of the strip set. Cut a 4" segment from the strip set. Repeat to cut a total of five 4" segments from the strip set.

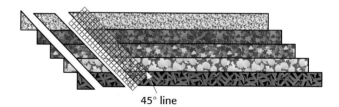

45° line

80

5 Cut five segments from each of the three remaining strip sets in the same manner, angling the ruler in the same direction as the stair-stepped ends of the strips.

6 Sew the right-angled strip segments together in pairs so that each complete strip will have a cloud fabric at one end and a green leaf print at the other end. Repeat for the left-angled strips.

7 Lay out the strips in alternating fashion, referring to the quilt assembly diagram. Notice that when the strips are sewn together the chevron design will form. Press the seams to one side.

8 To square up the zigzag edges of the quilt top, lay the quilt on your cutting table and align your rotary-cutting ruler so that the 1½" line intersects the top points of the blue tone-on-tone zigzags. Trim off the excess blue cloud fabric. Repeat for

the bottom of the quilt by aligning the 1½" line with the bottom points of the first floral fabric (sunflowers in our example). Trim off excess fabric.

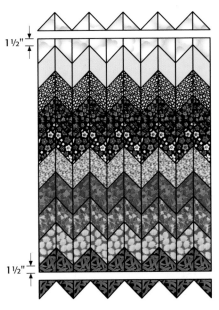

1½"

1½"

Trim top and bottom.

9 Measure the width of the quilt top. It should be approximately 35½". Trim the 4½" cloud fabric strip and the 4½" leaf fabric strip to this length. Sew the cloud strip to the top of the quilt and the leaf strip to the bottom of the quilt. Press the seams toward the newly added strips.

Borders

1 Sew three of the pink solid strips together end to end and press the seams to one side. From this long strip cut two border strips the same length as your quilt top, which should measure approximately 54½". Sew these strips to the sides of the quilt and press the seams toward the pink strips.

2 Trim the remaining two pink strips to the width of the quilt, which should be approximately 38½". Sew these strips to the top and bottom of the quilt and press the seams toward the pink strips.

3 Trim the two 6½" x 42" garden print border strips to the width of your quilt top (38½"). Sew these strips to the top and bottom of the quilt and press the seams toward the garden print fabric.

4 Measure the length of the quilt, which should be approximately 66½". Trim the two remaining 6½"-wide strips to this length. Sew the strips to the sides of the quilt and press the seams toward the garden print fabric.

Quilt Assembly

FINISHING

1 Cut the backing fabric into two equal lengths and sew the pieces together to make a backing with a horizontal seam. Trim the backing so that it is approximately 6" larger than the quilt top.

2 Layer the quilt top with the batting and backing; baste the layers together.

3 Hand or machine quilt as desired. Rosemary's quilt was machine quilted by Bronwyn Lane in a continuous-line flower design.

4 Trim the excess batting and backing fabric even with the edges of the quilt top. Join the garden print binding strips with diagonal seams and use them to bind the edges of the quilt.

5 Label your quilt and attach a hanging sleeve, if desired.

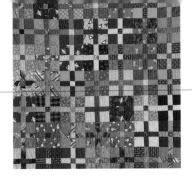

QUILTMAKING BASICS

Whether you're new to quiltmaking or you're simply ready to learn a new technique, you'll find this section filled with helpful information that can make putting your quilt together a pleasurable experience. Read through it now, or refer to it as needed for help with piecing, appliquéing, attaching borders, or finding the right tool for the job.

FABRICS AND SUPPLIES

Fabrics: Select high-quality, 100% cotton fabrics. They hold their shape well and are easy to handle.

Sewing machine: To machine piece, you'll need a sewing machine that has a good straight stitch. You'll also need a walking foot or darning foot if you are going to machine quilt.

Rotary-cutting tools: You will need a rotary cutter, cutting mat, and a clear acrylic ruler. Rotary-cutting rulers are available in a variety of sizes; some of the most frequently used sizes include 6" x 6", 6" x 24", and 12" x 12" or 15" x 15".

Thread: Use a good-quality, all-purpose cotton or cotton-covered polyester thread.

Needles: For machine piecing, a size 10/70 or 12/80 works well for most cottons. For machine quilting, a larger-size needle, such as a 14/90, works best. For hand appliqué, choose a needle that will glide easily through the edges of the appliqué pieces. Size 10 (fine) to size 12 (very fine) needles work well. For hand quilting, use "betweens," which are short, very sharp needles made specifically for this purpose.

Pins: Long, fine silk pins (with or without glass heads) slip easily through fabric, making them perfect for patchwork. Small ½"- to ¾"-long sequin pins work well for appliqué, although their shanks are thicker than silk pins.

Scissors: Use your best scissors only for cutting fabric. Use craft scissors to cut paper, cardboard, and template plastic. Sharp embroidery scissors or thread snips are handy for clipping threads.

Template plastic: Use clear or frosted plastic (available at quilt shops) to make durable, accurate templates.

Seam ripper: Use this tool to remove stitches from incorrectly sewn seams.

Marking tools: A variety of tools are available to mark fabric when tracing around templates or marking quilting designs. Use a sharp No. 2 pencil or a fine-lead mechanical pencil on lighter-colored fabrics, and use a silver or chalk pencil on darker fabrics. Chalk pencils or chalk-wheel markers make clear marks on fabric and are easier to remove than grease-based colored pencils. Be sure to test your marking tool to make sure you can remove the marks easily.

ROTARY CUTTING

Instructions for quick-and-easy rotary cutting are provided wherever possible. All measurements include standard ¼"-wide seam allowances. If you are unfamiliar with rotary cutting, read the brief introduction below. For more detailed information, see *Shortcuts: A Concise Guide to Rotary Cutting* by Donna Lynn Thomas (Martingale & Company, 1999).

1 Fold the fabric and match selvages, aligning the crosswise and lengthwise grains as much as possible. Place the folded edge closest to you on the cutting mat. Align a square ruler along the folded edge of the fabric. Place a long, straight ruler to the left of the square ruler, just covering the uneven raw edges of the left side of the fabric.

Remove the square ruler and cut along the right edge of the long ruler, rolling the rotary cutter away from you. Discard this strip. (Reverse this procedure if you are left-handed.)

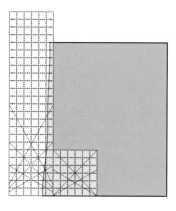

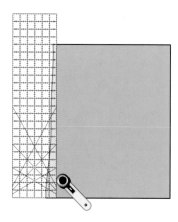

2 To cut strips, align the newly cut edge of the fabric with the ruler markings at the required width. For example, to cut a 3"-wide strip, place the 3" ruler mark on the edge of the fabric.

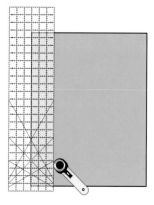

3 To cut squares, cut strips in the required widths. Trim the selvage ends of the strips. Align the left edge of the strips with the correct ruler markings. The sides of each square should have the same measurement as the width of the strips. Cut the strips into squares. Continue cutting squares until you have the number needed.

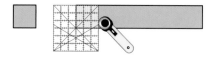

4 To make a half-square triangle, begin by cutting a square ⅞" larger than the desired finished size of the short side of the triangle. Then cut the square once diagonally, corner to corner. Each square yields two half-square triangles. The short sides of each triangle are on the straight grain of the fabric.

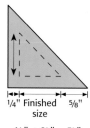

¼" Finished size   ⅝"

¼" + ⅝" = ⅞"

5 To make a quarter-square triangle, begin by cutting a square 1¼" larger than the desired finished size of the long edge of the triangle. Then cut the square twice diagonally, corner to corner. Each square yields four quarter-square triangles. The long side of each triangle is on the straight grain of the fabric.

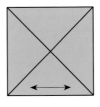
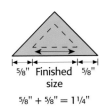

⅝" Finished ⅝"
size

⅝" + ⅝" = 1¼"

Machine Piecing

Most blocks in this book are designed for easy rotary cutting and quick piecing. Some blocks, however, require the use of templates for particular shapes, such as "Friendship Spools" on page 63. Templates for machine piecing include the required ¼"-wide seam allowances. Cut out the templates on the outside lines so that they include the seam allowances. Be sure to mark the pattern name and grain-line arrow on each template.

The most important thing to remember about machine piecing is that you need to maintain a consistent ¼"-wide seam allowance. Otherwise, the quilt blocks will not be the desired finished size. If that happens, the size of everything else in the quilt is affected, including alternate blocks, sashings, and borders. Measurements for all components of each quilt are based on blocks that finish accurately to the desired size plus ¼" on each edge for seam allowances.

Take the time to establish an exact ¼"-wide seam guide on your machine. Some machines have a special quilting foot that measures exactly ¼" from the center needle position to the edge of the foot. This feature allows you to use the edge of the presser foot to guide the fabric for a perfect ¼"-wide seam allowance.

If your machine doesn't have such a foot, create a seam guide by placing the edge of a piece of tape, moleskin, or a magnetic seam guide ¼" away from the needle.

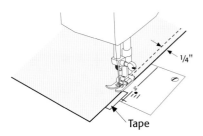

¼"

Tape

Chain Piecing

Chain piecing is an efficient system that saves time and thread. It's especially useful when you're making many identical units.

1 Sew the first pair of pieces from cut edge to cut edge, using 12–15 stitches per inch. At the end of the seam, stop sewing but do not cut the thread.

2 Feed the next pair of pieces under the presser foot, as close as possible to the first. Continue feeding pieces through the machine without cutting the threads in between the pairs.

3 When all the pieces are sewn, remove the chain from the machine and clip the threads between the pairs of sewn pieces.

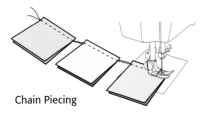

Chain Piecing

Easing

If two pieces being sewn together are slightly different in size (less than ⅛"), pin the places where the two pieces should match, and in between if necessary, to distribute the excess fabric evenly. Sew the seam with the larger piece on the bottom. The feed dogs will ease the two pieces together.

Excess

Pressing

The traditional rule in quiltmaking is to press seams to one side, toward the darker color wherever possible. First press the seams flat from the wrong side of the fabric; then press the seams in the desired direction from the right side. Press carefully to avoid distorting the shapes.

When joining two seamed units, plan ahead and press the seam allowances in opposite directions, as shown. This reduces bulk and makes it easier to match the seam lines. The seam allowances will butt against each other where two seams meet, making it easier to sew units with perfectly matched seam intersections.

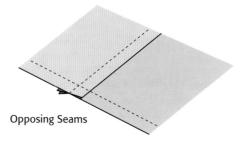

Opposing Seams

APPLIQUÉ BASICS

General instructions are provided here for needle-turn, freezer-paper, and fusible appliqué. Even when a specific method of appliqué is mentioned in a project, you are always free to substitute your favorite method. Just be sure to adapt the pattern pieces and project instructions as necessary.

Making Templates

To begin, you will need to make templates of the appliqué patterns. Templates made from clear plastic are more durable and accurate than those made from cardboard. And, since you can see through the plastic, it is easy to trace the templates accurately from the book page.

Place template plastic over each pattern piece and trace with a fine-line permanent marker. Do not add seam allowances. Cut out the templates on the drawn lines. You need only one template for each different motif or shape. Write the pattern name and grain-line arrow (if applicable) on the template.

Appliquéing by Hand

In traditional hand appliqué, the seam allowances are turned under before the appliqué is stitched to the background fabric. Two traditional methods for turning under the edges are needle-turn appliqué and freezer-paper appliqué. You can use either method to turn under the raw edges. Then use the traditional appliqué stitch to attach the shapes to your background fabric.

Needle-Turn Appliqué

1 Using a plastic template, trace the design onto the right side of the appliqué fabric. Use a No. 2 pencil to mark light fabrics and a white pencil to mark dark fabrics.

2 Cut out the fabric piece, adding a scant ¼"-wide seam allowance all around the marked shape.

3 Position the appliqué piece on the background fabric. Pin or baste in place.

4 Starting on a straight edge, use the tip of the needle to gently turn under the seam allowance, about ½" at a time. Hold the turned seam allowance firmly between the thumb and first finger of one hand as you stitch the appliqué to the background fabric with your other hand. Use a longer needle—a "sharp" or milliner's needle—to help you control the seam allowance and turn it under neatly. Use the traditional appliqué stitch, opposite, to sew your appliqué pieces to the background.

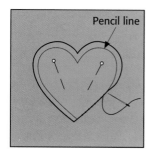

Pencil line

Freezer-Paper Appliqué

Freezer paper, which is coated on one side, is often used to help make perfectly shaped appliqués.

1. Trace around the template on the paper side (not the shiny side) of the freezer paper with a sharp pencil, or place the freezer paper, shiny side down, on top of the pattern and trace.

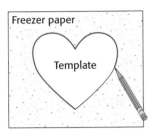

Freezer paper

Template

2. Cut out the traced design on the pencil line. Do not add seam allowances.

3. With the shiny side of the paper against the wrong side of your appliqué fabric, iron the freezer-paper cutout in place with a hot, dry iron.

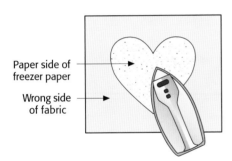

Paper side of freezer paper

Wrong side of fabric

4. Cut out the fabric shape, adding ¼" seam allowances all around the outside edge of the freezer paper.

5. Turn and baste the seam allowance over the freezer-paper edges by hand, or use a fabric glue stick. Clip inside points and fold outside points.

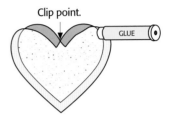

Clip point.

GLUE

6. Pin or baste the design to the background fabric or block. Appliqué the design using the traditional appliqué stitch, described below.

7. Remove any basting stitches. Cut a small slit in the background fabric behind the appliqué and remove the freezer paper with tweezers. If you used glue stick, soak the piece in warm water for a few minutes before removing the freezer paper.

Back of appliqué block

Traditional Appliqué Stitch

The traditional appliqué stitch or blind stitch is appropriate for sewing all appliqué shapes, including sharp points and curves.

1. Thread the needle with an approximately 18"-long single strand of thread in a color that closely matches the color of your appliqué. Knot the thread tail.

2. Hide the knot by slipping the needle into the seam allowance from the wrong side of the appliqué piece, bringing it out on the fold line.

3. Work from right to left if you are right-handed, or from left to right if you are left-handed.

4. To make the first stitch, insert the needle into the background right next to where the needle came out of the appliqué fabric. Bring the needle up through the edge of the appliqué, about ⅛" away from the first stitch.

5 As you bring the needle up, pierce the basted edge of the appliqué piece, catching only one or two threads of the edge.

6 Again, take a stitch into the background block right next to where the thread came up through the appliqué. Bring the needle up about ⅛" away from the previous stitch, again catching the basted edge of the appliqué.

7 Give the thread a slight tug and continue stitching.

Note: The stitches in the appliqué illustration are shown large to indicate placement. The stitches should not show in the completed work.

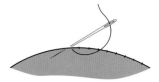

Appliqué Stitch

8 To end your stitching, pull the needle through to the wrong side. Behind the appliqué piece, take two small stitches, making knots by taking your needle through the loops. Check the right side to see if the thread shows through the background. If it does, take one more small stitch on the back side to direct the tail of the thread under the appliqué fabric.

Fusible Appliqué

Using fusible web is a fast and fun way to appliqué. If the appliqué pattern is directional, you need to make a reverse tracing of the pattern so the pattern will match the original design when fused in place. Otherwise, your finished project will be the reverse of the project shown in the book. You don't need to make reverse tracings for patterns that are symmetrical or for ones that are already printed in reverse, such as the heart pattern for "Crazy Hearts" on page 39.

Refer to the manufacturer's directions when applying fusible web to your fabrics; each brand is a little different and pressing it too long may result in fusible web that doesn't stick well.

1 Trace or draw your shape on the paper-backing side of the fusible web. Cut out the shape, leaving about a ¼" margin all around the outline.

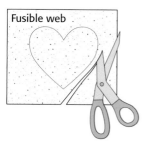

Fusible web

2 Fuse shapes to the wrong side of your fabric.

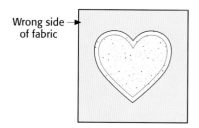

Wrong side of fabric →

3 Cut out the shape exactly on the marked line.

4 Remove the paper backing, position the shape on the background, and press it in place with your iron.

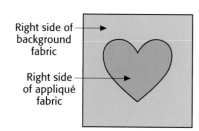

Right side of background fabric →

Right side of appliqué fabric →

ASSEMBLING THE QUILT TOP

From squaring up your blocks to make them easier to sew together, to adding borders that aren't wavy, you'll find all you need to know about assembling your quilt top here.

Squaring Up Blocks

When your blocks are complete, take the time to square them up. Use a large square ruler to measure your blocks and make sure they are the desired size plus an exact ¼" on each side for seam allowances. For example, if you are making 9" blocks, they should all measure 9½" before you sew them together. Trim the larger blocks to match the size of the smallest one. Be sure to trim all four sides; otherwise your block will be lopsided.

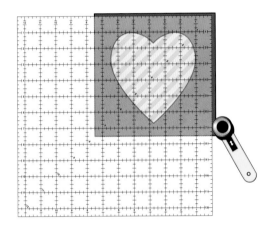

If your blocks are not the required finished size, adjust all the other components of the quilt, such as sashing and borders, accordingly.

Making Straight-Set Quilts

1 Arrange the blocks as shown in the quilt assembly diagram included with the project instructions.

2 Sew the blocks together in horizontal rows, pressing the seams in opposite directions from one row to the next.

3 Sew the rows together, making sure to match the seams between the blocks.

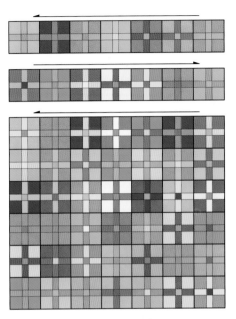

Straight-Set Quilt

Making Diagonally Set Quilts

The following steps describe how to sew together a diagonally set, or on-point, quilt.

1 Arrange the blocks, side setting triangles, and corner setting triangles as shown in the quilt assembly diagram provided with each quilt.

2 Sew the blocks and side setting triangles together in diagonal rows, pressing the seams in opposite directions from row to row.

3 Sew the rows together, making sure to match the seams between the blocks. Sew the corner setting triangles on last.

Side setting triangle

Corner setting triangle

Diagonally Set Quilt

Adding Borders

For best results, do not cut border strips and sew them directly to the quilt without measuring first. The edges of a quilt often measure slightly longer than the distance through the quilt center, due to stretching during construction. Instead, measure the quilt top through the center in both directions to determine how long to cut the border strips. This step ensures that the finished quilt will be as straight and as "square" as possible, without wavy edges.

Many of the quilts in this book call for plain border strips. These strips are cut along the crosswise grain and seamed where extra length is needed.

Borders may have butted corners, corner squares, or mitered corners. Check the quilt pattern you are following to see which type of corner treatment you need.

Borders with Butted Corners

1 Measure the length of the quilt top through the center. From the crosswise grain, cut two border strips to that measurement, piecing as necessary. Determine the midpoints of the border and quilt

top by folding in half and creasing or pinning the centers. Then pin the borders to opposite sides of the quilt top, matching the center marks and ends and easing as necessary. Sew the border strips in place. Press the seams toward the borders.

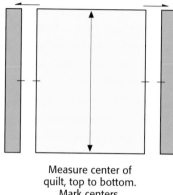

Measure center of quilt, top to bottom. Mark centers.

2 Measure the width of the quilt top through the center, including the side borders just added. From the crosswise grain, cut two border strips to that measurement, piecing as necessary. Mark the centers of the quilt edges and the border strips. Pin the borders to the top and bottom edges of the quilt top, matching the center marks and ends and easing as necessary. Sew the border strips in place. Press the seams toward the border.

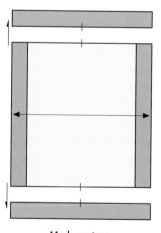

Mark centers.
Measure center of quilt, side to side, including border strips.

Borders with Corner Squares

1 Measure the width and length of the quilt top through the center. From the crosswise grain, cut border strips to those measurements, piecing as necessary. Mark the center of the quilt edges and the border strips. Pin the side borders to opposite sides of the quilt top, matching centers and ends and easing as necessary. Sew the side border strips to the quilt top; press the seam allowances toward the border.

2. Cut corner squares of the required size, which is the cut width of the border strips. Sew a corner square to each end of the remaining two border strips; press the seam allowances toward the border strips. Pin the border strips to the top and bottom edges of the quilt top. Match centers, seams between the border strips and corner squares, and ends. Ease as necessary and stitch. Press the seam allowances toward the borders.

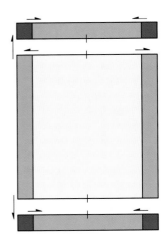

Borders with Mitered Corners

1. Estimate the finished outside dimensions of your quilt, including the borders. For example, if your quilt top measures 35½" x 50½" across the center and you want a 5"-wide border, your quilt will measure about 45" x 60" after the borders are attached. Add at least ½" to these measurements for seam allowances. To give yourself some leeway, you may want to add an additional 3" to 4" to those measurements. In this example, you would then cut two borders that measure approximately 48" long and two borders that measure approximately 63" long.

Note: If your quilt has multiple borders, you can sew the individual border strips together first and treat the resulting unit as a single border. When mitering the corners, take care to match up the seam intersections of the multiple borders.

2. Fold the quilt in half and mark the centers of the quilt edges. Fold each border strip in half and mark the centers with pins.

3. Measure the length and width of the quilt top across the center. Note the measurements.

4. Place a pin at each end of the side border strips to mark the length of the quilt top. Repeat with the top and bottom borders.

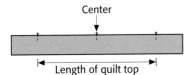

Center

Length of quilt top

5. Pin the borders to the quilt top, matching the centers. Line up the pins at either end of the border strip with the edges of the quilt. Stitch, beginning and ending the stitching ¼" from the raw edges of the quilt top. Repeat with the remaining borders.

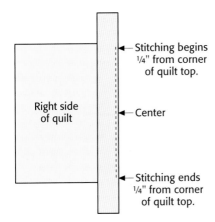

Right side of quilt

Stitching begins ¼" from corner of quilt top.

Center

Stitching ends ¼" from corner of quilt top.

6. Lay the first corner to be mitered on the ironing board. Fold under one border strip at a 45° angle to the other strip. Press and pin.

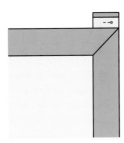

7 Fold the quilt with right sides together, lining up the adjacent edges of the border. If necessary, use a ruler and pencil to draw a line on the crease to make the stitching line more visible. Stitch on the pressed crease, sewing from the corner to the outside edges.

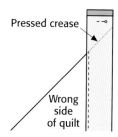

Pressed crease

Wrong side of quilt

8 Press the seam open, check the right side of the quilt to make sure the miters are neat, then turn over the quilt and trim away the excess border strips, leaving a ¼"-wide seam allowance.

9 Repeat with the remaining corners.

PREPARING TO QUILT

If you'll be quilting your project by hand or on your home sewing machine, you'll want to follow the directions below for marking, layering, basting, and quilting. However, if you plan to have a professional machine quilter quilt your project, check with that person before preparing your finished quilt in any way. Quilts do not need to be layered and basted for long-arm machine quilting, nor do they usually need to be marked.

Marking the Quilting Lines

Whether you mark quilting designs on the quilt top or not depends upon the type of quilting you will be doing. Marking is not necessary if you plan to quilt in the ditch (along the seam lines) or outline quilt a uniform distance from seam lines. For more complex quilting designs, however, mark the quilt top before the quilt is layered with batting and backing.

Choose a marking tool that will be visible on your fabric and test it on fabric scraps to be sure the marks can be removed easily.

See "Marking tools" on page 83 for options. Masking tape can be used to mark straight quilting lines. Tape only small sections at a time and remove the tape when you stop at the end of the day, or the sticky residue may be difficult to remove from the fabric.

Layering and Basting the Quilt

Once you complete the quilt top and mark it for quilting, assemble the quilt "sandwich," which consists of the backing, batting, and the quilt top. The quilt backing and batting should be about 4" to 6" larger than the quilt top all the way around. Batting comes packaged in standard bed sizes, or it can be purchased by the yard.

For large quilts, you may need to sew two or three lengths of fabric together to make a backing. Trim away the selvages before piecing the lengths together. Press the seams open to make quilting easier.

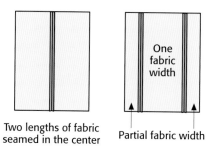

One fabric width

Two lengths of fabric seamed in the center

Partial fabric width

1 Spread the backing wrong side up on a flat, clean surface. Anchor it with pins or masking tape. Be careful not to stretch the backing out of shape.

2 Spread the batting over the backing, smoothing out any wrinkles.

3 Center the pressed quilt top on top of the batting. Smooth out any wrinkles and make sure the quilt-top edges are parallel to the edges of the backing.

4 For hand quilting, baste with needle and thread, starting in the center and working diagonally to each corner. Then baste a grid of horizontal and vertical lines 6" to 8" apart. Finish by basting around the edges. For machine quilting, baste the layers with #2 rustproof safety pins. Place pins about 6" to 8" apart, away from the areas you intend to quilt.

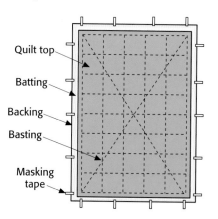

Quilt top

Batting

Backing

Basting

Masking tape

QUILTING TECHNIQUES

Some of the projects in this book were hand quilted, others were machine quilted, and some were quilted on long-arm quilting machines. The choice is yours!

Hand Quilting

To quilt by hand, you will need short, sturdy needles (called betweens), quilting thread, and a thimble to fit the middle finger of your sewing hand. Most quilters also use a frame or hoop to support their work. Use the smallest needle you can comfortably handle; the finer the needle, the smaller your stitches will be. The basics of hand quilting are explained below. For more information on hand quilting, refer to *Loving Stitches: A Guide to Fine Hand Quilting* by Jeana Kimball (That Patchwork Place, 1992).

1. Thread your needle with a single strand of quilting thread about 18" long. Make a small knot and insert the needle in the top layer about 1" from the place where you want to start stitching. Pull the needle out at the point where quilting will begin and gently pull the thread until the knot pops through the fabric and into the batting.

2. Take small, evenly spaced stitches through all three quilt layers. Rock the needle up and down through all layers, until you have three or four stitches on the needle. Place your other hand underneath the quilt so you can feel the needle point with the tip of your finger when a stitch is taken.

3. To end a line of quilting, make a small knot close to the last stitch; then backstitch, running the thread a needle's length through the batting. Gently pull the thread until the knot pops into the batting; clip the thread at the quilt's surface.

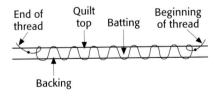

End of thread   Quilt top   Batting   Beginning of thread

Backing

Machine Quilting

Machine quilting is suitable for all types of quilts, from wall hangings to crib quilts to full-size bed quilts.

Marking the quilting design is only necessary if you need to follow a grid or a complex pattern. It is not necessary if you plan to quilt in the ditch, outline quilt a uniform distance from seam lines, or free-motion quilt in a random pattern.

For straight-line quilting, it is extremely helpful to have a walking foot to help feed the quilt layers through the machine without shifting or puckering. Some machines have a built-in walking foot; other machines require a separate attachment.

For free-motion quilting, you need a darning foot and the ability to drop or cover the feed dogs on your machine. With free-motion quilting, you guide the fabric in the direction of the design rather than turning the fabric under the needle. Use free-motion quilting to outline quilt a fabric motif or to create stippling or other curved designs.

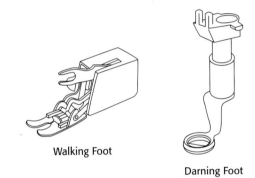

Walking Foot

Darning Foot

Long-Arm Machine Quilting

If you prefer to have your quilt quilted by a professional, ask at your local quilt shop for references about someone in your area who does this type of work. Generally, for long-arm quilting, you don't layer and baste the quilt prior to giving it to the quilter, nor do you have to mark the quilting designs. Check with your long-arm professional to be sure of specifications regarding batting and backing sizes before cutting or piecing yours.

FINISHING

Bind your quilt, add a hanging sleeve if one is needed, label your quilt, and you're finished!

Binding

For a double-fold binding, cut strips 2" to 2½" wide across the width of the fabric. (Some quilters prefer narrow binding, especially if a low-loft batting is used. If you're using a thicker batting, you may want to use 2½" strips.) You will need enough strips to go around the perimeter of the quilt, plus 10" for seams and to turn the corners.

1 Sew the binding strips together to make one long strip. Join strips at right angles, right sides together, and stitch across the corner, as shown. Trim excess fabric and press the seams open to make one long piece of binding.

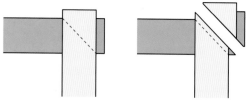

Joining Strips

2 Fold the strip in half lengthwise, wrong sides together, and press.

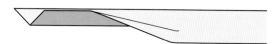

3 Trim the batting and backing even with the quilt top. If you plan to add a hanging sleeve, do so now before attaching the binding (see page 96).

4 Starting near the middle of one side of the quilt, align the raw edges of the binding with the raw edges of the quilt top. Using a walking foot and a ¼"-wide seam allowance, begin stitching the binding to the quilt leaving a 6" tail unstitched. Stop stitching ¼" away from the corner of the quilt.

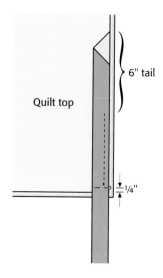

Quilt top

6" tail

¼"

5 Lift the needle out of the quilt, then turn the quilt so you will be stitching down the next side. Fold the binding up, away from the quilt, with raw edges aligned. Fold the binding back down onto itself, even with the edge of the quilt top. Begin stitching ¼" from the corner, backstitching to secure the stitches. Repeat the process on the remaining edges and corners of the quilt.

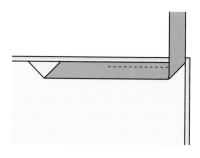

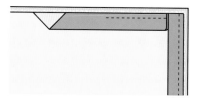

6 On the last side of the quilt, stop stitching about 7" from where you began. Overlap the ending binding tail with the starting tail. Trim the binding ends with a perpendicular cut so the overlap is exactly the same distance as the cut width of your binding strips. (If your binding strips are 2½" wide, the overlap should be 2½"; for 2"-wide binding, the overlap should be 2".)

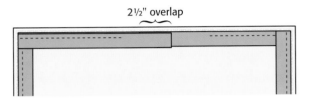

2½" overlap

7 Open up the two ends of folded binding. Place the tails right sides together so they join to form a right angle, as shown. Pin the binding tails together, then mark a diagonal stitching line from corner to corner.

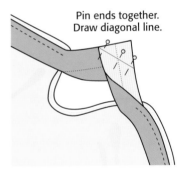

Pin ends together.
Draw diagonal line.

8 Stitch the binding tails together on the marked line. Trim the seam allowance to ¼"; press the seam open to reduce bulk. Refold the binding, align the edges with the raw edges of the quilt top, and finish sewing it in place.

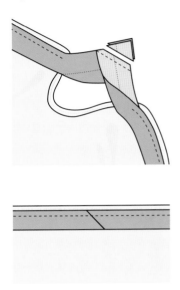

9 Fold the binding to the back of the quilt top to cover the machine stitching line. Hand stitch in place, mitering the corners.

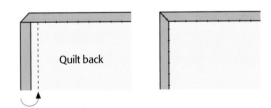

Quilt back

Hanging Sleeve

If you plan to display your finished quilt on the wall, be sure to add a hanging sleeve to hold the rod.

1. Using leftover fabric from the quilt backing, cut a strip 6" to 8" wide and 1" shorter than the width of your quilt. Fold the ends under ½", then again ½" to make a hem. Stitch in place.

2. Fold the fabric strip in half lengthwise, wrong sides together, and baste the raw edges to the top of the quilt back. The top edge of the sleeve will be secured when the binding is sewn on the quilt.

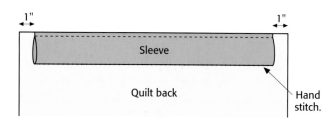

1"

1"

Sleeve

Quilt back

Hand stitch.

3. Finish the sleeve after the binding has been attached by blindstitching the bottom of the sleeve in place. Push the bottom edge of the sleeve up just a bit to provide a little give so the hanging rod does not put strain on the quilt.

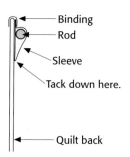

Binding
Rod
Sleeve
Tack down here.
Quilt back

Signing Your Quilt

Future generations will be interested to know more than just who made it and when, so be sure to include the name of the quilt, your name, your hometown and state, the date, the name of the recipient if the quilt is a gift, and any other interesting or important background about the quilt. The information can be handwritten, typed, or embroidered.